HEALING FOR THE EMPTY HEART

HEALING FOR THE EMPTY HEART

MARION DUCKWORTH

BETHANY HOUSE PUBLISHERS
MINNEAPOLIS, MN 55438

Published by Bethany House Publishers
A Ministry of Bethany Fellowship, Inc.
11300 Hampshire Avenue South, Minneapolis, Minnesota 55438

Printed in the United States of America

Library of Congress Cataloging-in-Publication Data

Duckworth, Marion.
    Healing for the empty heart / Marion Duckworth.
        p.   cm.
    Includes bibliographical references.
    1. Christian women—Religious life. 2. Women—Religious life. 3. Christian life—1960–   I. Title.
BV4527.D834   1993
248.8'43—dc20   93-4359
ISBN 1–55661–314–8   CIP

To the Counselor

MARION DUCKWORTH is an award-winning author with ten books, numerous curriculum materials, and over four hundred published articles to her credit. She has traveled extensively while leading Abiding Ministry retreats, seminars and workshops. She is the past president of the Oregon Association of Christian Writers. Marion and her husband have three grown children and make their home in Oregon.

Contents

Healing for the Empty Heart

I

The Starting Place

1

Running on Empty

My friend Cathy was recalling her experience of several years before.

"Something's wrong with me—that's what I kept telling myself," she reminisced.

"I didn't know what. But something was definitely wrong. For one thing, I was depressed and I cried a lot, especially when I went to bed at night. I was so unhappy."

I nodded, understanding fully. That's how it had been for me. Emotions raw. A perpetual frown inside my head. Guilt that I couldn't shake off.

Like Cathy, the vague but penetrating uneasiness that shadowed me is gone now, and after much healing I can speak about the chasm of emptiness I'd carried inside me all those years.

In my earliest years, I had developed a distorted view of who I was and about my place in the world. This skewed view resulted in thoughts that were out of sync with what was true—thoughts that became an engine of painful emotions, driving me into behavior that I hated.

Here was the hardest part: Conversion to Christ, and subsequent spiritual experiences with God, made very little real difference. True—I knew that I knew God. And I knew that I'd go to heaven when I died. But still those haunting words pounded me from within: *Something's wrong with me.*

Since, I've met hundreds of women who felt the way I did. They, too, whispered to God, *"Something's wrong with me."* Finally, in desperation, many of them have cried out the same one-word prayer that I did: *"Help!"*

We who have been to pain and back want to assure you of one important fact: *You can count on God to answer that prayer. Absolutely.*

Right now you may be frightened because of the way you feel. Perhaps you think, *It's hopeless. I don't have what it takes to become the woman I want to be.* I assure you that damaged women can experience healing from the vast emptiness inside. I'll also explain, step by step, how the healing process takes place.

I was scheduled to talk to women in a church on this subject and was making arrangements with the pastor's wife on the phone. She said with conviction, "You may not agree with me, but I believe we're all damaged."

Dr. David Seamands has written: "It does not matter how nearly perfect the home life or the mental and physical inheritance. Because we live in the kind of world we do, each of us bears emotional scars."[1]

Sometimes we're not sure what has caused the internal wounds, in the same way we're not sure how we got a small bruise. All we are sure of is that we hurt. Mostly we keep silent about the pain, the way I did. *I shouldn't be this way. I'm a Christian.*

No, we may not know exactly what's wrong, but we do know—only too well—how we feel and how we fail. Here's

[1]David A. Seamands, M.A., D.D., *Healing for Damaged Emotions* : (The Narramore Christian Foundation, 1969), pp. 5–6.

how a few of the many women I've met describe themselves:

"I have all these fears. It's not any one thing—I guess you could say I have *fear*. I'm afraid I'll leave the stove on, or the house unlocked. I have to check and double-check."

"I have this problem with food, and I feel so ashamed and guilty."

"I'm *angry*. I hate myself for not feeling differently toward certain people—but I can't stop, and I feel guilty."

"I get so depressed. Sometimes I feel as though it isn't worth making an effort to stay alive."

"I keep getting into destructive relationships with men. After each one, I feel more beat up, put down, and ashamed."

"My nerves are so on edge that I snap at my husband and verbally abuse my children. I feel like a shrew."

"Either I'm overly sensitive and cry, or I get offended easily. I can't seem to change."

Beneath It All

Underlying all of these emotions is a deeper state of being, and that is *emptiness*. For many of us, there was a great emotional void into which fell our painful feelings. What we wanted from life and from those around us was love and a sense of well-being. Our souls were tender and young and open, and we looked for the *good thing* to fill us.

For too many of us, however, vari-shaped miseries filled those new, young souls, causing overwhelming pain and causing us to despair that life could ever be anything *but* hurtful. And so, the deep emptiness that lies beneath the false bottom of our souls is rooted in our past.

Some women, for instance, experienced denigration or dehumanizing acts. When our fathers, brothers, or uncles should have been reading us *Winnie the Pooh,* they were crawling beneath the covers and doing shameful things to our bodies. Or we were ignored, rejected, or emotionally abandoned by our parents or husbands. Or we longed to be held and hugged by our daddies who, instead, were busy hugging a bottle. Instead of having mothers who built us up, we were smacked down. When we should have been children, we found ourselves having to be parents. Tension was so strong in our home that it tightened the muscles in our necks and sickened our stomachs.

Or perhaps the reasons for our emptiness are more subtle, built into the messages our brains recorded: *Why can't you be like your sister?* Or, *We expect you to accomplish great things. We expect you to excel.* Maybe the message was implied and never spoken: *Around here we never talk about feelings.* Or, *You are a disappointment to me.*

Let's face the plain facts, too. Perhaps the problems were no one's *fault.* Daddy died and Mama fell apart. Or Mama was stricken with mental illness, causing her to act like a stranger. Perhaps our particular personality made us more sensitive than others. Or our interpretation of events may have darkened our souls in ways no one suspected.

Whatever our pain, the reason *behind* the reasons is the same: People live and move and try to have their being in a sinful world. Sin causes every one of us to think and act distortedly. As a result, and often without meaning to, we slash one another. Often the wounds that result are so deep and wide that they don't heal.

Helen, who was sexually abused, has wandered in and out of a series of devastating relationships with men who were themselves damaged.

Eileen, whose parents were damaged themselves and unable to love and affirm her, has become a rigid, perfectionistic Christian, trying to earn the favor of God and man.

Growing Up Empty

Personally, I learned to be overly responsible when I was growing up. I was the only child of a mother with a heart condition and other serious ailments and a father who was mentally ill and had been institutionalized since I was two years old. My home would be described today as *dysfunctional* because I was the caretaker.

When I was in junior high, we lived in a basement apartment in Coney Island, on a government "dole," hundreds of miles from any of my mother's family. Since Daddy was Jewish and Mama was a Christian, our Jewish family and neighbors mostly treated us as outsiders.

For months life would be fairly smooth. I'd go to school, and Mom would keep house and ride the streetcar for a nickel each way to the surplus food station to bring home cornmeal, butter, and beans. She'd cook our meals, drink tea, and rest and sit next to me in the big chair while we listened to radio programs.

But then she'd have a heart attack and have to go to the charity ward of a hospital. Pale and weak upon release, she'd get herself home by subway and trolley, nearly stumbling down the basement steps to our apartment and into bed. And there she'd have to stay—sometimes for weeks. This is how I became Mama to my mama.

Recently, during a post-Christmas housecleaning, I found old letters Mama had written to one of her sisters some forty years ago. In one of them, she described my routine when she was ill: "She [does] all the shopping, cooking, cleaning, washing, and serves me in bed and keeps up with schoolwork."

When I grew up, I came to believe that I was responsible for the well-being of every person in my world, in the same way I had been responsible for the most important person in my childhood. Becoming a Christian only compounded my problem, for pastors and evangelists convinced me I was responsible for the soul of everyone I knew. If I did not witness to them and they wound up in hell, it would be my fault.

Was the empty pit in my soul Daddy's fault? Mama's fault? My fault?

No. It was the result of living in the kind of world we do. Everyone and everything in it is irregular.

I have memories about imperfect and irregular things. Sales of irregular merchandise make bargain-hunters tingle with anticipation. On sunny Saturday afternoons, Mama and I loved to walk the avenue in Coney Island, browsing in sidewalk-sale bins. Once she bought me a blouse and skirt we found for a nickel each because they were faded. Mama "fixed" the clothing by bleaching it so it was all one color, and we celebrated our wonderful purchase.

On Sunday afternoons soon after my marriage to John, in New York City, we'd walk through the bargain district of downtown Manhattan. Outside the immigrant mom-and-pop grocery stores, we'd peer into bins of dented canned goods: tomatoes, green beans, peaches—all greatly reduced. Cash was scarce, but we never bought these goods. *Maybe the peaches, beans, and tomatoes were spoiled because they were dented.*

About thirty years later, in the Pacific Northwest where John and I now live, we began shopping at a food warehouse. I wasn't overly enthusiastic the first time I pushed a cart down their aisles, though, because although prices were cheap, the cans of food I wanted were dented—"irregulars."

By now, my husband had learned the truth. "Dents don't affect what's inside. Just don't pick ones that have serious dents where they're sealed."

I leaned on his logic and took home some tomatoes and

peaches. They were delicious. The food warehouse became one of my favorite places to shop.

But one afternoon as I browsed its aisles and stopped to examine a tower of dented cans, I had a flash of insight. *The whole world is a food warehouse and most of us are damaged goods. We were whacked and smacked in the soul early on, or dented later.* In my mind's eye in place of cans, I saw so many of the women I knew, standing side by side, built up into a human tower.

We are not tin cans, turned out on a factory assembly line. We have a brain that remembers and feelings that hurt. The damage doesn't merely wound our exterior, leaving our insides intact.

We are dented on the inside as well. The damage may not show in our faces, but inside we're writhing or steeling ourselves or fighting futility. Our interior wounds affect the way we think about ourselves, about God, about others. They color the way we decide, behave, and live our lives.

The Great Physician

I limped, damaged and hurting, through my earlier Christian days, crying "help" to God because I thought, *Something is wrong with me.* Even though I knew God heard my prayers, He didn't seem to be answering. I felt as though I'd stumbled into an emergency center, only to find it empty—all the skilled, caring people gone, the corridors silent.

But day after day, I kept my heart open to God. I didn't know where else to go. I didn't know this was actually the key to healing.

Much later, I would understand: As soon as I cried out to God, He heard! And not only did He hear me, He began to maneuver me to the place and the circumstances best suited to expose my empty, empty insides—and to begin the healing process.

Healing for the Empty Heart

One day last year, I was sitting quietly, talking to God about the many women who'd been coming to me because of their own wounds and sense of emptiness. I was reflecting on Bible passages, wanting to give wise spiritual help to these women, and I came across these words of Jesus: "I will ask the Father, and he will give you another Counselor to be with you forever. . . . He . . . will be *in* you" (John 14:16–17, NIV, emphasis added).

God is our Counselor. God himself. That's one of the reasons He's come to live in us. To fill us and heal us on the inside. God Almighty, Maker of heaven and earth, has chosen to come and live in us and become our "primary-care physician." He wants to be the Counselor of every hurting woman.

It is because of Him that many women, my friend Cathy and I included, have gone on to experience healing. Yes, the process takes time. And yes, it means walking through pain to come to peace. But beyond any doubt I can tell you, there is wholeness. You will not be transformed from sobs to smiles tomorrow morning at eight o'clock. But gradually, God does bring beauty out of ashes.

For so many people today the healing process involves getting help from other people. Trained professionals can play an important role in our lives, and so can support groups. When they are proficient, advisers and groups are God's gift, as countless thousands can attest.

But the core of our healing is this:

God himself is our divine Counselor—our primary-care physician. He is the one who initiates and oversees our entire healing process. The word translated *Counselor* in the New

International Version of the Bible comes from a word that means "one who comes with strength."[2]

He is "one called in to stand by and give aid," as Bible commentator Kenneth Wuest explains.[3] This means that God is our

- Comforter
- Helper
- Intercessor
- Advocate
- Strengthener
- Standby (John 14:16, the Amplified Bible).

The very day you became a Christian, God came into your life to be your divine Counselor. He *wants* to heal you and fill you on the inside, and He has been waiting for you to realize that you need healing.

God, the Missing Piece

Yes, there is a lot written about healing these days. Certainly, the needs of hurting people are great. But as Christians we do a disservice if, in helping people to find relief from psychological and emotional pain, we fail to bring them into healing contact with the One whose presence is the missing piece they *most* need to make them whole.

Yes, your healing, like that of many others I know, will be the result of a cooperative process—God and you working together with others. He'll use a variety of people, tools, and experiences—like friends, human counselors, and support groups. Healing does not, perhaps cannot, take place in a vacuum. He'll help you privately, when you are alone, through prayer, journaling, and meditating on Scripture.

[2]Kenneth S. Wuest, *Wuest's Word Studies in the Greek New Testament, Vol. III* (Grand Rapids, Mich.: Wm. B. Eerdman's Publishing Co., 1973), p. 90.
[3]Ibid., p. 91.

Take a moment and think about it.

God wants to heal you and fill you with himself.

That was one great aspect of His mission when He came to earth.

The moment you ask, He begins to work on your behalf.

He will never give up on you. When you think the emptiness is too deep a void for Him to heal, He will comfort and reassure you. When you need shoring up, He's there to strengthen you. The psalmist knew:

> He guides the humble in what is right and teaches
> them his way. (Psalm 25:9)

That doesn't mean that He merely guides us in the moral way to live—how to spend our money and relate to the neighbor whose tongue is a sharpened stick. The biblical principle that David gives us here applies also to the right way in which we should see ourselves, to interpret our experiences and to live in freedom.

Pat, who hid behind closed drapes in her house week after week, knows it. Because of the Counselor, she has walked out the door, down the street, and into life.

Joan, who was convinced she was unlovable, knows it. Because of the Counselor, she knows she is loved and is at peace with herself.

Laura, who'd spent her life running away from memories of a childhood ruled by alcoholic parents, knows it. Because of the Counselor, she is at rest.

"The Father . . . will give *you* another Counselor to be with *you* forever. . . . He . . . will be in you" (John 14:16–17, emphasis added).

He has come to oversee *your* healing and infilling.

Believe it. It's true.

Thinking It Over

1. If you have ever felt that something is wrong with you, when have those feelings been strongest?
2. To which of the descriptions of a damaged woman in this chapter do you most relate?
3. Do you agree that each of us bears emotional scars? Why or why not?
4. Have you believed before that God wants to be your primary-care physician and heal your wounds? What new thoughts on the subject come to mind now?
5. Review the names of God in this chapter from the Amplified Bible version of John 14:16. What aspects of the Holy Spirit as our healer of wounds does each name show?

2

Learn How to Trust

During the long, long years that I cried out to God for help, I thought I needed a spiritual quick-fix—a one-shot dose of spiritual power.

Mainly I was convinced I had a spiritual problem.

I'm not close enough to God, I thought. So I would pray, *I surrender, Lord. I die to self. Fill me with your Spirit so I can live a victorious Christian life.*

If I could only bend low enough and pray hard enough, I thought God would reward me by filling my emptiness with love, joy, and peace instead of fear, despondency, and insecurity. All my pleadings were based on the premise that even though I was a Christian I was still bad and, therefore, a perpetual beggar before the throne. My mind was slammed shut against any other idea because fear and despondency were "sinful." So every morning, I crawled before the Presence like a faceless, generic servant—cringing and begging for forgiveness. I was also hoping and praying for a wave of God's wand, a sweeping of His Spirit. Then I backed away to perform my tasks.

Sooner or later on in the day or the week, though, I'd crumble before a harsh word, or avoid a task that required risk, and cry or hide or close up hard and cold. Following that, I'd silently scream at myself: *Failure, failure—FAIL-URE!* Then I'd drop to my knees before God, and the miserable process would begin all over.

Like so many women I've met since, I was caught in a destructive behavior cycle from which there seemed to be no out. It went in a cycle, like this: Guilt . . . shame . . . blame . . . compensation . . . defeat . . . guilt . . . shame.

Most hurting women play a variation on the same theme:

"I'm so angry at my mother for controlling my life all these years that I eat to feel better."

"My dad blamed me for my mother's death. So now I carry around a ton of guilt, and it makes me feel as if I have to do everything perfectly."

"Even minor confrontations leave me shaking, because I grew up in a war zone, not a family. I hide inside myself."

"I grew up in one foster home after another and never had real love. Maybe that's why I have an affair, see it end, and have another."

It's as though we've been diagnosed with a fatal disease and the only treatment we know is, at best, ineffective. But we feel so caught in our pain and the resulting sinful behavior—and yet we dare not stop for fear of falling into that pit of despair and emptiness. It seems impossible to believe there is any way out.

But God gently urges us to trust Him to take us down the journey to freedom. "Come to me, all you who are weary and burdened, and I will give you rest" (Matthew 11:28).

"Come . . ."

Rest.
One of the first steps I had to take was to stop compul-

sively taking on tasks—like marching elephants, trunk-to-tail—first this, then this, then that. For so long, work made me feel worthwhile—at least a little—so I continued on like a robot.

We want to stop our coping mechanisms, but that would leave us out there, standing emotionally naked in the cold, with nothing to protect us from the fearsome void.

"*I want* to lose weight," a woman at a retreat confided. "But my fat is my protection. It keeps people away. Then they can't hurt me." She suspected that God wanted to help dissolve that protective layer, just as I suspected at an early stage in my healing that God wanted to teach me to rest in Him, instead of filling my time and my soul with accomplishments. What was lacking was the key ingredient for rest—and that was *trust.*

Like nearly everything else in life, trust is something we learn. "Childlike faith" is no exception. A woman's image of God is based largely on the qualities of her father. Author Heather Harpham puts it this way: "Imagine that you were given a blank canvas at birth. Your father's words and actions (or lack thereof) provided the tools, paints, and brushes with which you could paint an image of God as you grew up. What color God did you paint?"[1]

For me the color was dark and foreboding. I believed that my biological father had deserted me. *Back-of-the-brain* insisted that was true because an adult authority figure once told me Daddy had *chosen* to become sick—though now I know that was not true.

Daddy didn't care enough about me to stay well was the message. So I concluded that God, who is called the Father, must be untrustworthy, too. Daddy hadn't been there to hold me on his lap and tend my bruises. How could I expect

---

[1]Heather Harpham, *Daddy, Where Were You?* (Lynnwood, Wash.: Aglow Publications, 1991), p. 129.

God to be that kind of Father?

Many of the women I've talked with paint the same kind of picture. Tanya was young and attractive and very active in her church. After a retreat, I loaned her a copy of my first book, *The Greening of Mrs. Duckworth,* which describes my own recovery. When I asked how she was progressing, she said, "Fine. But I skipped over one chapter."

"Which one?"

"The one that's titled 'God.' "

It's not just God whom we eye with suspicion. Those of us who've been damaged in the past look at other people with cautious eyes as well. Women have admitted to me that when they are in a room with a man they don't know well— even if there are others present and even in a church—they stiffen inside. The message they are sending: *Don't try to get close to me.*

Why? *He's a man, so he's a threat,* is the way they reason— for they are seeing men now through the experiences they had in the past when they were hurt or abandoned.

It's not that we don't have the *potential* to trust. We're born with the ability and we do so every day. Involuntarily, we count on the pharmacist to prepare the correct prescription and the mail carrier to deliver important documents. More often than not our trust is rewarded.

But if when we were small and defenseless, big people said one thing and did another, or hurt us when they should have helped, the tender shoots of trust were trampled instead of cultivated. Therefore, we need to think first about what trust and faith are all about so that spiritual growth can take place now, in adulthood.

Pistis is the Greek word for faith. It means primarily "firm persuasion, a conviction based upon hearing."[2] The

---

[2] W. E. Vine, *The Expanded Vine's Expository Dictionary of New Testament Words* (Minneapolis, Minn.: Bethany House Publishers, 1984), p. 401.

apostle Paul puts it this way: "Faith comes by hearing the message . . ." (Romans 10:17).

That's what I had to do when my youngest son, Mark, came home from a trip to the coast with friends and showed me a scrape on his leg. "There was this dog—and he tried to bite me."

A dog bite? And I had no idea if the animal was diseased or not?

It didn't seem to be a puncture wound. Our long-time family physician administered a tetanus shot and said we didn't need to do anymore so long as it didn't get worse.

The next week or so, I wondered. Suppose the doctor was wrong. Suppose the bite was more serious than he thought, or the dog had rabies and Mark was infected.

Daily, I watched the wound as it healed. When the scar developed red spots, I felt a tinge of worry. But I chose to put my faith in the doctor's words—in his message—and not in my feelings. He'd proven himself capable and trustworthy as our family physician for decades. He was versed in medicine and I wasn't. Mark recovered nicely.

When it comes to counting on God to be our Counselor, we're not trusting the words of fallible men. The statements come directly from the infallible, inspired Word of God. Although we may be unsure, insecure, afraid—still we are called to make a choice to commit ourselves to God, our Physician and Counselor. We are called to do so, not based on what we *feel,* but on what we *know*—or what we *can* know if we take the first step of faith. Feelings are important, but they do not have to motivate what we do. It's what we *know* that should motivate our behavior.

Here is what we know:

1. *God wants to be a perfect father to us and to restore our damaged soul to wholeness.*

"He heals me. . . . He is like a father to us, tender and sympathetic to those who reverence him" (Psalm 103:3, 13, TLB).

2. *God wants to love us on the inside.*

"May you be able to feel and understand . . . how high [God's] love really is; and to experience this love for yourselves" (Ephesians 3:18–19, TLB).

3. *God's ability to heal us is unlimited.*

"Understand how incredibly great his power is to help those who believe him. It is that same mighty power that raised Christ from the dead" (Ephesians 1:19–20, TLB).

4. *God always does what He says He will do.*

"[Christ] carries out and fulfills all of God's promises" (2 Corinthians 1:20).

These words are God's words to the one whose trustability has been damaged:

"I will heal you. I want to be a tender, sympathetic father to you. I love you unendingly. I have absolute power to heal and restore. I always keep my promises."

I had to make a choice to trust God—at the head of my own crisis. On a Sunday afternoon I took my sorrow out the door and down the sidewalk along a main thoroughfare.

As I walked, sobbing, I sensed that the Lord of that unhappy day and all the other days of my life silently and inwardly posed a question: *"Will you trust me, even though you don't understand what I am doing?"*

The next moment I found the answer erupting like a tender shoot from the soil of my soul: *"Though he slay me, yet will I trust him."* Job's words, spoken on an ash heap, had become my faith response.

On the corner of the next block, I walked into a fast-food place and solemnized my declaration of faith-without-sight over a paper cup of coffee. God was God, and that was a fair beginning.

Faith Is Growth

The choice to trust God is just the beginning. Contrary to many notions, God doesn't usually regenerate us, heal us, and call us to full-time ministry in one dramatic moment. Faith and trust are living, growing things.

Once we have made a *choice* to trust God, He leads us through the *process* by which faith in Him becomes personal. He also leads us through the process by which we learn to trust ourselves and people who are deserving of it.

Learning trust, after we have taken a step of faith, is part of our healing process. And it *is* a process. Why doesn't God *zap* us whole instead—heal all our dents by a sweep of His divine Spirit? After all, can He not raise the dead?

Once in a while, God does heal like that. Most of us have heard of men and women from whom God has instantly removed the desire for a destructive substance and ever afterward they were changed.

More often, healing comes gradually. Why? We were created to be learners. Think of it: When we were born, we knew how to do only a few things instinctively—like suck, cry, sleep. Everything else we've had to learn.

Every human being born on this earth is a learner. Even Jesus, who—although He was the Son of God—was also a real human being. He had to learn to feed himself, walk, talk, use a saw, and do the myriad other things that were part of life in His world.

Our progress as learners may seem like that of the inch-worm. Not because God can't instantly heal, but because the gradual learn-and-grow process is the marrow of the human race.

The first time around, we may have learned wrongly what it means to be an individual—whole and valuable. Now, we're relearning, and that takes time. That we can really change at all may seem impossible. *My wounds pierce clear through my soul. They can never be healed.*

A pastor was sure that a tiny tree outside his church was done for: "I came one Sunday morning and found that this tree the preschool kids had planted was broken off. Only a slim strand of fibers remained intact." He straightened it up, thinking it would at least look okay for that day. "But I had no hope that it would survive." With three preaching services each Sunday morning and a schedule full of appointments, he forgot about the tree. It wasn't until a year or so later when he drove by it that he stopped and stared in amazement. "The little tree was not only intact—it was in full bloom."

Cherry Boone O'Neill, a victim of eating disorders, felt that becoming a survivor was just as impossible for her. "I likened myself to an intricately designed, fine gold chain that had become badly tangled in knots. [My doctor] helped me straighten the chain, and together [my husband] and I were beginning to untie the knots. I had come so close to throwing it all away."[3]

To be healed, we need to know exactly what's wrong with us. "First . . . the root cause of the matter must be brought up from the lower, unconscious level. . . . Only then can the Holy Spirit heal the wound, as only he can do," says David Seamands.[4]

Insight comes in a variety of ways. One of the first times

---

[3]Cherry Boone O'Neill, *Starving for Attention* (N.Y.: Dell, 1982), p. 197.

[4]David A. Seamands, M.A., D.D, *Healing for Damaged Emotions* (The Narramore Foundation, 1969), p. 14.

for me was an afternoon when I got out of my car and began to walk across the parking lot to the door of a supermarket. Standing by the door was a cluster of young men, talking with one another. Fear made my mind dart for other ways to get into the store. *I'm afraid to go past them.* But another part of me chided, *This is nonsense. You're a grown woman, a wife, a mother—and a missionary, of all things.* Although I was still ill at ease, I forced myself to walk past them and into the store.

For days after, the memory of that experience troubled me. Why had I felt hot with embarrassment as I made my way past those young men to purchase eggs and milk? That's when I recalled other times of shame in high school. I'd been afraid to pass clusters of boys on street corners because I was sure they were laughing at me. Now the *something's-wrong-with-me* feeling became more specific: I knew I was afraid of rejection.

That was confirmed in the months ahead. In the rural community where my husband was pastoring, I felt responsible to call on women I didn't know and to establish relationships. But I was terribly afraid. When I knocked on a door, would the lady of the house stand, unsmiling, speak in grudging monosyllables, and stare at me? Would she say, "I'm too busy to visit with you," close the door, and leave me standing on the porch alone and rejected?

Over a period of time, I came to see *why* I was afraid of rejection. The way I interpreted messages from people and from circumstances during my early life added up to an inner message that ran over and over in the back of my mind: *You are worthless.*

Women ask me, "How long did it take you to get over your past? Did you backslide during the process? I've experienced some healing, but I still have problems relating to God. Why can't I get over this?"

Of course we will slip back. Like yours, my thought patterns and emotions are conditioned responses. They are learned reactions. New situations trigger them—and old reactions can begin to take over, if I let them.

For years, new authority figures were intimidating—even though I knew they shouldn't be. But as I made my way forward, I began to recognize "warning" thoughts and feelings of impending pain for what they were. I came to see that these old ideas were no longer appropriate: They were not truth. So I no longer needed to allow them to control me. Gradually, those thoughts and the feelings they generate eased and I was able to allow truth, based on healthy new experiences, to motivate my behavior. And if we will not trust—expecting that sometimes we will be knocked, but not broken—we will never begin to heal.

Trust means testing life, and testing people, and learning what is safe and what is not. This is a process that never stops. And in our spiritual journey with God, we come to Him by faith, place our trust in Him, and learn that—though He does not always do exactly what we want, on our time schedule—He *is* trustworthy.

Nor should we expect to become perfectly balanced personalities. Some days we will be more ambitious than others, some days more determined, some days more emotional. Distorted ways of thinking—such as, "My father pretended normalcy but slammed and snarled behind the shades, so no man can be trusted"—may be woven into our psyches. Restoration is a delicate process.

An illustration of the God-superintended healing process can be seen in the restoration of Michelangelo's frescos in the Vatican's Sistine Chapel. After their completion in 1512, their original beauty was gradually covered by a veil of grime, including pollutants like soot and grease from burning candles as well as wine used to try to clean the frescos.

These masterworks were vanishing. Because "Scabs of glue [had] fallen away, pulling pigment with them," it was decided that restoration was essential.[5] The director of art history of the Vatican museum was in charge.

Did the four restorers expect to use household cleanser on so irreplaceable a subject, and to toss off the job in a week? Hardly. "The restorer's credo is like the physician's: First, do no harm."[6] Slowly, carefully, using the best scientific methods, they began.

It was months before some of the luster of artistic genius, as it had come from the master's brush, began to show through. *Nine years* from the day the workers began, the restoration was complete. Today, visitors to the chapel can stare in wonder at the stunning sweep of beauty made new.

To God, we are each a masterpiece—a priceless creation. He aches to begin His work, both through the Holy Spirit and the restorers He brings into our lives. With gentle tenderness and divine confidence, He will persevere.

Our part is to commit the restoration process to Him and to choose to cooperate, despite the pain. For many of us our greatest pain will come as we risk and, in risking, learn to trust again. If we do, we'll find ourselves evolving from victim, to survivor, to victor, to comforter of others.

Count on it.

Thinking It Over

1. When something happens to make you feel rejected or afraid, what do you do to feel better? Has this action proven to be constructive or destructive? Explain.
2. If there was a person during your growing-up years who

---

[5] David Jeffery, "A Renaissance for Michelangelo," *National Geographic* (December 1989), p. 697.
[6] Ibid.

betrayed your trust, in one sentence describe how he or she did it. If there was more than one, write a sentence about each. Identify ways you think those experiences may have affected your ability to trust God.

3. In spite of the way you may feel, write a letter to yourself explaining why you *know* God can be trusted. Based on Psalm 102:11–13, Ephesians 3:18–19, Ephesians 1:19–20, 2 Corinthians 1:20, what are some things He wants to do for you? Read from the Living Bible, if possible.

4. After being afraid to walk past a group of young men in front of a supermarket, the author's feeling that "something's wrong with me" became more specific. She knew she felt afraid because she'd been rejected in the past, and her ability to trust had been eroded. What experiences in your past may be the root causes that have promoted fear and feelings of rejection in you?

5. Reread the illustration of the restoration of Michelangelo's frescos at the end of Chapter Two. Describe yourself as a priceless work of art based on Psalm 8:3–9. Think of as many similarities as you can between the work of the restorers of the frescos and God's work in you.

3

Damaged Women Speak

A couple I'll call the Smiths began their marriage in a dream home with surrounding gardens—a gift to them that was absolutely debt free. But they made some tragically wrong choices, lost their jobs—the ones for which they'd been ideally suited—and as a result had to leave town. In their new location, they had to sweat for a living.

That's when their two sons came along. The senior Smiths tried to make the best of life in the present tense. Nevertheless, the family always seemed to be living in the shadow of life in the past tense.

The older son grew up to be a farmer and the younger a rancher who seethed toward his more devout brother. *Why should he get all the admiration from Mom and Dad, and not me?* Jealousy bred resentment, and resentment brought a craving for revenge. Cunningly, he coaxed his brother out into a field, where he attacked and killed him.

So you've caught on. This is really Adam and Eve and Cain and Abel—the first "dysfunctional family."

When I called that fact to the attention of a woman you'll meet in this chapter, she laughed. "I guess I thought dysfunctional families were a product of modern times."

Hardly. Remember Lamech who bragged to his wives that he murdered a man for injuring him? (Genesis 4:19–24). Can you imagine what life would have been like with *him* for a father?

Remember Hagar, a single mom, who took her son Ishmael and ran away because she was being so badly abused by Sarah, for whom she worked as a servant? (Genesis 16). How would you have liked to grow up in that home the way Ishmael did?

Remember Jacob—one of a pair of twins whose parents played favorites? Isaac, who had a yen for roasted game, loved Esau, who was a skillful hunter. Rebekah loved Jacob, who stayed at home with her. That unhealthy beginning left a mark on the twins (Genesis 25:19–34; 27).

These biblical characters were definitely *not* filling their roles the way God intended. Like them, families have been out-of-whack since humanity was stung with the venom of self-centeredness when the serpent struck in Eden. Since the same poison remains in the universal human system, we have the same potential to cause and to experience pain.

In this chapter, real women who have been damaged and healed tell their stories. The accounts contain much more, however, than a rehearsal of their miseries, for they also describe their own growth process in order to give you hope and help.

God will not work exactly the same way in your life as He did in theirs. Don't try to copy their experiences. Instead, we'll identify key, transferable truths that you can prayerfully hold in your heart.

Jennifer's Story

A beautiful and accomplished woman in her late thirties, Jennifer causes heads to turn. Few know the pain she carried for so long.

"I don't think I ever saw my father sober until about ten years ago. For the first few years of my life, my grandmother raised me. She was very loving and I was well-treated by my aunts, uncles, and cousins."

But when she was still a preschooler, Jennifer was thrust back into her parents' home. "It was very violent. Dishes crashed and chairs were thrown. The sudden change from a nurturing environment terrified me.

"My grandmother had taught me to talk to Jesus as though He were my friend and was right there with me, and sometimes I did." That habit may have saved Jennifer's life the time her dad hauled her into the car and took off even though he was too drunk to drive. "I asked Jesus to give me strength to take the wheel even though I was petrified to do it. But I knew I had to steer to stay alive."

Besides the trauma of her father's alcoholic behavior, Jennifer suffered physical, emotional, and verbal abuse from her mother.

"I'd walk into a room and she'd haul off and slap me in the face or knock me against a wall for no apparent reason." She was told over and over that she wasn't as good as others— that "I wasn't normal"—because she was quiet and liked to read. "There's something about being slapped in the face that causes a lot of shame. So I grew up with a deep, deep sense that something about me was just *wrong*."

She kept wondering: *Is there something wrong with me?* "My extended family assured me there wasn't—but that there was something wrong with my mother and father. My aunt even confronted my parents about their abuse." But Jennifer still was not convinced that the problem wasn't in her.

As a twelve-year-old, she went to the police and reported the abuse. "The captain just looked at me with disbelief. And that was the end of that." She had risked, and when the man she thought would protect her did not respond, her ability to trust was even more impaired.

In her late teens she went for counseling because, even though she'd won awards and contests, she still felt terribly inadequate. It cost too much money, though, so she didn't go back.

At eighteen, Jennifer signed up for a course in drug and alcohol counseling in college. "The interviewer asked if living with an alcoholic parent affected me. I told her that it hadn't because I was a Christian and had overcome it with the Lord." During training and internship she was required to go through counseling herself—and she found out differently.

When Jennifer was asked to imagine that she was a child again talking to her father, her response was unexpected. Now she recalls the experience: "It was a flood of emotion. I was shocked at how much I'd pushed down—and how much he'd hurt me.

"But I had come to understand that alcoholism is a progressive disease and affects people. My dad didn't know what he was doing half the time." As a result, she says, it was fairly easy to forgive him.

"After a period of time—out of the blue—I started being very angry with my mom. I'd see scenes in my mind of when I was a little girl and she'd throw a pail of water on my head. I tried and tried to choose to forgive her. But the anger didn't go away." The emotional stress was exhausting Jennifer, and she was becoming depressed. That's when she heard about a Christian counseling center and entered for inpatient treatment.

During therapy, Jennifer relived her terror and anger toward her mother. "I remembered being in bed when I was about ten. My mother came in and hit me for no reason. The counselor prayed, and Jennifer the child began to forgive. "It was like a weight lifted," she says. Before she left, a pastor prayed with her through the stages of her life. Jennifer would call up scenes from the past, and ask the Lord to help her come to rest through forgiveness at each one.

She returned home after two and a half weeks, knowing that she still needed to talk with someone who'd understand. A friend recommended that she call me, and we met for several months, during which time Jennifer talked in detail about her early life—especially about her mother—something she had never done until her recent treatment. "It's like tying up the loose ends," she told me.

Jennifer's relationship with her mother is slowly healing, and she's begun telling her story to groups of women and helping them come to terms with painful matters long buried.

Caroline's Story

"About six years ago, I began to gain insight into what was wrong with me. That's when I responded to an invitation to invite Jesus into my life."

Caroline had been sexually abused by several males: a family member, male baby-sitters, and her own father. The latter began about the time she entered puberty. "Finally, I figured out ways to keep him away from me," she says. "What he did then was to turn to my sisters. He made my life miserable by showing them massive preference and setting us against one another so we couldn't be friends. He was also extremely critical.

"For me to get good grades was very important to him, but when I did bring home straight A's, he didn't acknowledge them at all." She wanted his approval but found no way, except with sex, to get it. And that was out of the question.

Caroline's mother suspected that she was being sexually

abused by someone outside the family, but didn't check it out. "Mom claimed she never knew Dad was abusing me or my sisters. Dad was really hard on her during that period, and I felt as though she relegated her wifely role to her daughters."

Years later, two of Caroline's nieces told school authorities that their grandfather (Caroline's dad) had been sexually molesting them. Amazingly, the court never even questioned Caroline or her sisters to see if he'd sexually abused them, too. He received four years probation, went through counseling with three psychiatrists, and remained in denial.

Caroline explains: "I'd been depressed on and off for years and found myself on a merry-go-round. It went like this: A doctor prescribed valium for a back ailment I had. That made me depressed; then they'd prescribe antidepressants. I'd get more depressed because I couldn't handle my anger. Then I began to drink to numb my feelings.

"I decided to put myself in a drug and alcohol treatment program as an outpatient. Part of the commitment was to go to at least two AA meetings a week. With each step, I got stronger.

"After I was in that program for six months, I was directed into a sexual abuse recovery program. They'd wanted me to be stabilized before I went into more painful stuff. All these programs were secularly based. And the private counselor I saw was not a Christian."

Soon after, Caroline married a man she thought was a Christian. She found out quickly that not only was he *not* a Christian, he was abusive as well. "I'd thought marrying him would be a way to get one part of my life secure." He would not change, and soon they were divorced.

Caroline entered a secular group-therapy program that provided further healing. Then one of her sisters who'd also been sexually abused by her father confronted him. "He just laughed in her face," Caroline says. "It was as though all the years of counseling and therapy I'd had were for nothing. I was right back in the pain I thought I'd gotten rid of. The anger, bitterness and hatred."

Caroline was now a Christian, and to survive she reached out to her church and began attending small-group Bible studies. "I started learning what love was in the spiritual sense—and that was something I'd never known. Until then, I'd seen God the way I saw my father. Strict. Unloving. Now I was learning that Jesus wanted to love me and sur-round me with love. A lot of that didn't make sense, and I had to do some soul-searching.

"I'd just figured that love meant giving in to men. If they slept with me that meant they loved me. I didn't realize, until I got into my spiritual walk with God, that that's not love at all. That's strictly lust—a taking."

One well-meaning Christian woman was a major hin-drance. "She was very forthright and expected me to be able to simply forgive and go on. If I didn't, she told me God wouldn't use me." Although the woman did have the ability to confront, she did it without tact or wisdom.

Caroline did find help. "These days I have no need for pills or alcohol to numb-out. I know I can deal with my memories and feelings differently. One way is through my church, which is like a spiritual family. Then God also brought a retired pastor and his wife into my life, and they've become like my adopted parents. For a while, I was uneasy around him simply because he's a man and I've been uncom-fortable around men.

"But just knowing there is someone I can call if I feel as though I can't handle things—that helps. I don't have to go through a receptionist. It's made a big difference. This couple is centered in God, and they give me scriptural guidance. I've never known what it feels like to have a mom and dad. I'm actually starting to feel normal."

Comfort From Friends

If Jennifer and Caroline had the chance to sit across the table from you over tea, they'd take your hand and urge you to follow the Holy Spirit, the Counselor, toward healing.

In the next chapters, I'll describe some of the means He uses. Read the pages prayerfully, asking Him to show you which you should do *now,* so you can get in touch with and express the feelings you have suppressed, leaving an empty vacuum inside. You will also discover root causes for your hurt—and learn new ways to think, feel, and act.

For now, would you pray this prayer, trusting the Counselor to hear you?

I am not alone.

Other women have experienced similar pain. I can be made whole. I know that you, Holy Spirit, my Counselor, will superintend a healing process tailor-made for me. I choose to cooperate with you.

Thinking It Over

1. At what point did Jennifer and Caroline feel that *something's-wrong-with-me* sense? When did you?
2. What words does each woman use to describe her painful feelings? What words would you use to describe yours?
3. If you were either woman's friend, what advice would you have given her when she was struggling? How would you respond if someone gave you that advice?
4. In the beginning, each woman tried to quell the inner

turbulence in different ways. What were they? Why were they ineffective?

5. What specific people, groups, and events did God use at various stages to contribute to each woman's healing? How does that encourage and instruct you?

II

The Healing Journey

4

Find Human Help

No matter how much we coaxed, the cat simply would not come out from behind the television set. "It's pretty humiliating," I told my husband, "to be hated by a cat."

John and I were visiting our son Paul and his new wife, Cher, in Florida. Situated in a corner of the living room was their television set—and behind it, almost from the beginning, hid the cat.

"Astro never does this," Cher apologized, trying to pull her out by one leg. But the cat, determined to stay in hiding, made herself leaden.

Finally, Astro the cat-hermit began to show signs that her behavior might be more than a fear of strangers. A vet confirmed what Paul and Cher suspected: Astro was sick, and she'd been hiding because she felt so terrible.

Don't we sometimes handle our pain the same way—by hiding, and crying silently to ourselves and God? It's hard enough to be real and honest in the privacy of our soul to an unseen God. It's enormously harder for many of us to reveal an aching heart to another *person.*

But that's what we need to do. When it came to telling

a *person*, I dug in my heels and made myself leaden, because I supposed that revealing my secret pain would also reveal that I was a stunted Christian. Besides, I'd have to talk about other people in my life and that would be disloyal. I'd expose myself as "weird." I wouldn't know what to say. And when the words finally did come out, they'd be slathered with tears. Anyway, ripping myself open and revealing my insides was too big a risk. Would I be belittled or believed? Chastised or cared for?

"Safe" Friends

Since we are learning how to live all over again, it's important that we learn to open ourselves to the right people in the right ways. Yes, it is vital that we speak out of our inner selves to another of our species, because God has planned to use human vessels to help unravel the tangles of our lives. But to whom shall we go? Who is safe?

Our natural instinct is to go to someone who is *supposed* to be safe.

The first person Angie thought of was her husband. "I kept saying that I needed help, and didn't know whom to see or what to do. My husband didn't know what to tell me or how to advise me.

"My best friend was in the middle of a divorce. I knew that the advice she gave me was colored by her own experiences and wasn't trustworthy." Angie couldn't talk to her parents—they were part of the problem, as is often true.

Many women find it difficult to open up. And if the first person they choose can't relate, they find it even harder to try again. Some women are inherently articulate and have no trouble verbalizing what's going on inside. The trouble is, they may tell too many people, and people who cannot help anyway. For women like this, *telling* is cathartic for today—but tomorrow the pain returns. Then they must find someone else to tell. Instead of being constructive, this kind of telling is futile and leads away from healing rather than toward it.

Often a woman will find the right compassionate friend. In addition, there's a second person she may need to tell as well: her family doctor. For one thing, a variety of medical problems affect our moods. Psychologist Dr. William Davis says that physiological causes for emotional problems can include: "a hormone imbalance, a viral illness, the result of toxicity such as an overdose of some medication. A lot of metabolic changes can cause a person to be depressed." At one stage of my life, I felt terrible emotional stress cyclically. When I realized it was premenstrual tension, I saw my physician and received help.

I recommend that you have regular checkups with a physician, and if troubles persist get other professional opinions.

In addition to treating physical causes, your physician may recommend that you see a professional counselor and may even suggest someone. Suppose, though, you had a medical checkup recently and were pronounced physically healthy. Your doctor didn't recommend that you see a counselor, but your internal problems have not gone away. If they keep plaguing you—go for help.

For Angie, reaching for help was urgent. "I couldn't say a sentence without getting my words tangled. My emotions were raw. I cried easily and started thinking of how I could die.

"I was having problems at work and knew that my co-workers knew it. Things reversed themselves in my mind, and I couldn't say what I wanted to say. I just plain lost it."

On her daily commute home from work, Angie listened to a Christian talk show. A Christian counselor from a nearby city was a frequent guest, and people would call in and talk about their problems. "I called the counselor I heard on that program and got the name of a Christian counselor in my city. I called him for an appointment and saw him regularly for a year." Through the contact, she was helped.

Unfortunately, a considerable number of women I meet aren't sure it is acceptable for a Christian to go for professional therapy. Jennifer, whose story is told in Chapter 3, says, "I was told that since I was a Christian, I didn't need to see a counselor." Others have families who strenuously object.

Writing about her own experiences twenty years ago, Joan Jacobs tells us, "Twice recently someone has said, 'You don't need a psychologist when you have the Bible.' "[1] At least in some Christian circles, that mind-set remains the same. She strongly disagrees with that premise. "It may well be that reading the Bible shows a person his need for professional care. In verse after verse we are confronted with God's standard, the awesome fact that we 'should be holy and blameless before him.' How do we move forward to *that* standard? Some of us find ourselves faced with problems that block our growth in spite of prayer, Bible study, worship, and fellowship."[2]

Dr. Davis says he usually asks people in this situation, "If you needed a bypass, would you refuse to go for surgery and pray for healing? Or would you go for surgery and pray as well?" He draws a parallel between the knowledge of the cardiologist and the counselor. Another clinician points out that Jesus was concerned with the whole body, and the mind is part of the body.

It is the exception and not the rule for God to make us instantaneously whole. More likely He will use the human

---

[1] Joan L. Jacobs, "The Christian and the Head-Spreader," *Christianity Today* (Feb. 1, 1974), p. 4.
[2] Ibid.

specialists He has provided. For He did create mankind to live interdependently. Ultimately, of course, all healing comes from God. Our personal responsibility is to do whatever is necessary to become healthy in body, mind, and spirit. And that means going to helpers whom God has placed in this world when that's necessary. Give yourself permission to do so.

Besides asking your family doctor, you can also ask your own pastor or one in a large, respected church in your area for names of counselors they recommend.

You may wonder what kinds of professional therapists there are to choose from. Here are a few:

- a psychiatrist: also a medical doctor; in addition to giving therapy, he or she can prescribe medication
- a psychologist: does testing, diagnosis, assessment, and therapy
- a clinical social worker: gives therapy and emphasizes the assimilation of the individual into society
- a counselor: gives therapy, which should include practical steps for working out and resolving conflict

A psychologist is probably a good person with whom to start. Competent clinicians won't be shy about referring you to someone else if necessary. You may want to call your mental health agency to find out if counselors are required to be licensed in your state. In mine, they are not. "One day they can be a plumber and the next a counselor," a professional told me. Be wary of untrained, self-styled counselors—even Christian counselors.

Is it acceptable to go to a non-Christian for therapy? One woman I met in another state decided she needed to see a professional—only to discover there were no Christian counselors in her area. She contacted me and asked that very question. "Is it okay to see a non-Christian?"

In my opinion, it is preferable to see a Christian counselor *if he or she is on a professional par with a non-Christian.* If you choose a non-Christian, however, ask the person who recommends him whether or not he proselytizes toward his world view. You have a right to interview any counselor beforehand. Most professionals will allow you to do that over the phone—some in person. Ask whatever you'd like to know that's pertinent about the counselor and the process. Your questions ought to bring satisfactory responses about

—educational background

—experience with similar cases, and the success rate

—the kind of therapy he or she ordinarily uses with that kind of problem, and the treatment plan once assessment has been made

—the fee, and how payments may be made

—if the counselor is a non-Christian, will he or she work within your value system?

—if the counselor is a Christian, does he or she believe the Bible is God's Word, Christ is the Son of God and our Savior, the Holy Spirit is the indwelling Counselor and Guide?

—limits of confidentiality

—how will he or she interact with other family members?

For some women who are uncomfortable with men because of past experiences, a female counselor may be preferable. "I chose a woman because she felt safe," a friend told me.

After the first visit, you'll probably sense whether or not he or she is someone with whom you feel comfortable. *Good rapport is essential.* "If the client doesn't feel trust, a sense of well-being and hope, he or she probably needs to go elsewhere," Dr. Davis explains.

On the other hand, I've met women who have seen one therapist after another. The reason one gave was simple enough: "He didn't care about me." If that behavior becomes a pattern, it may be time to ask yourself, "What's going on here? Am I choosing carelessly? Or are my expectations unreasonable?"

Christian treatment centers that provide in-patient care are helpful for those who are having trouble handling day-to-day life. Jennifer arranged for a two-week stay in one when her anger toward her abusive mother became overwhelming. One benefit of such treatment is that the individual receives twenty-four-hour care and is freed from the day-to-day stress of the outside world while she does the inner work that assists in healing. Investigate ahead of time to learn what you need to about the treatment team and the specific program. Usually there is private psychiatric and/or psychological counseling in addition to group therapy. Medical consultation should also be available if necessary.

Such treatment centers are located throughout the United States. The nature of the therapy varies from program to program, so it is best to get specific information to see if the one you're interested in meets your needs. A particular center may focus on special problems as well.

A center should provide a safe environment, where clients feel accepted. It should also have a good record of effectively treating emotional problems and related disorders. Look for one that uses the most modern methods available and is scripturally based and Christ-centered.[3]

Many women I know have gone without help because they had no medical insurance or money to pay for professional counseling. In that situation, find out which of the

---

[3]Two such facilities that offer inpatient care are:
Minirth-Meier Clinic 1–800–545–1819
RAPHA 1–800–227–2657

counselors recommended to you has a sliding-fee scale that adjusts to your income and resources. If you can't afford that, contact your county mental health department for names of private, nonprofit centers or public facilities.

Charitable organizations like the Salvation Army and the United Way may be able to provide information as well. Perhaps your city has a hot line, or a drop-in counseling center. You'll find it listed in the Yellow Pages. Another option is to call large churches in your area for information. They may have counseling facilities themselves or be able to put you in touch with no-charge or minimal-charge counseling centers.

Your Local "Shepherd"

Is a pastor a viable choice as a counselor? That depends. Some pastors I know are especially gifted in this helping ministry, and they devote a significant amount of time to that purpose. The pastor you have in mind may be schooled and gifted in that area—or he may not. It's unreasonable to expect every minister to be trained and adept in every area. Does he have a reputation as a counselor who's helped people over the long-term?

Dr. Davis suggests that you ask yourself (if you are already seeing a pastor or another counselor): "Am I being helped?" True, the counsel may feel uncomfortable—but it should not make you feel more guilty, afraid, ashamed, or unstable. Beware of counsel like that.

Trish was far too shy to talk in depth to her pastor. When an older woman spoke at her church women's group and mentioned guilt, Trish indicated in an offhanded remark during discussion time that *she* had tons of experience with it.

After the meeting, the speaker approached Trish and

asked if she'd like to get together and talk. That's what they did, and gradually Trish became convinced that here was someone who understood. This new friend had experienced some of the same anxiety, and had self-doubt and learned how to cope with it. The woman turned out to be a helping friend, with lay-counseling experience. Some churches have trained lay counselors available, and you can approach one. Or you may be able to talk with a pastor's wife, or another mature Christian.

Here are some simple rules of thumb:

A truly *helping* friend will not preach to you, criticize you, or heap advice on you. They will be an active listener— one who really *hears* what you say and draws you out. They will suggest alternative actions and pray with you for direction from God. They may share from their own experiences and gently direct you to passages in Scripture that provide insight—but never insist that you do exactly what they did to find relief.

If you are already seeing a professional counselor, a helping friend can also work with you to accomplish personal daily goals like staying on task and structuring your day. Let's say you need exercise. Maybe your friend will go with you for a walk. Do you need nourishing food in the house but are too depressed to get it? A friend may go with you to the supermarket and help you make choices. No true friend will *take over.* Instead, he or she will come alongside, the way God himself does.

The majority of women I know who have reached for the option of professional help have had positive experiences. A few have not. "[A counselor] may foster dependency—particularly with depressed women," Dr. Davis says. Dogmatic counseling that gets people into a submissive pattern is destructive.

"The clinician is not going to fix the damage," Davis

continues. "There's nothing miraculous about counseling. I don't read minds or have a magic wand. Rather, I see myself as in the business of teaching people how to do their own therapy. I tell people that you can't take me home in your back pocket; you have to figure out how to do this yourself. If I facilitate them in learning how to think through a particular kind of problem, I'm doing my job."

Here's one woman's description of how that works: "The counselor helped me listen to what my heart was feeling. . . . A good counselor will listen carefully without passing judgment, counseling can help people like me quit criticizing themselves long enough to hear their own needs. And needs are not faults."[4]

You will want to know periodically where you are in the counseling process and what needs to be done next. Not that your human helper will be able to chart out a trip ticket from brokenness to wholeness. We are living humans and our responses along the way can't be precisely predicted.

Except for one. When it hurts, we'll flinch and want to draw back. *I want to go home. Get me out of here.* This is a common response to feeling suppressed pain. Pulling away from pain is normal—but facing pain is also one of the greatest challenges to getting better. Like the accident victim who must face painful physical therapy or remain crippled, we must push through barriers of pain that have bound us too long.

Here is our hope: If we will walk through the valley of restoration, we will come into the wider, sunnier place of health.

And restoration does cause pain. Count on it. Just last evening a woman sat on my sofa blotting her tears. "I can't remember when I've cried this much." Why? "Because touching the wounded places hurts and releases painful

---

[4]"How Counseling Helped Me, One Woman's Story," *Discipleship Journal*, Issue Fifty, 1989, p. 25.

thoughts and feelings," I told her. "Until you let yourself feel what's inside and express those feelings, there's no room for the love you want so badly."

During my own walk toward health, I often felt like a five-year-old boy whom I heard about recently. When he was told to take a bath, he wished for a pet giant to work for him—then *he* could be as lazy as he wanted.

A nice idea. But neither God our Healer nor our counseling helper is our pet giant. Healing isn't something that happens *to* us through the people to whom we delegate that responsibility.

Healing only happens *in* us as we ourselves walk through the pain and toward the hope that is held out before us. Remember that we don't go alone. God our Counselor goes with us, healing our wounds and filling our emptiness, just as He promised. That is our hope.

Thinking It Over

1. Do you find it easy to talk about your feelings or not? What do you think are the reasons?

2. What advice does Galatians 6:2 give? According to Galatians 6:3, what is one criteria for a confidante? What other criteria do you have?

3. When is the last time you had a physical checkup? Might physiological problems like digestive upsets, insomnia, PMS and menopause be contributing to the way you feel? What action do you need to take?

4. How would you choose a counselor? What would you say to someone who argued that going for counseling is wrong for a Christian?

5. What are some things a counselor could do for you? A helping friend?

5

Support Groups

If I could do anything over from my misery years, it would be to push pride out the door, pick up the phone and keep calling until I found someone who could help me. I was a most-hesitant traveler on the road to health.

I did make a feeble attempt to get help when I called a pastor and made an appointment. He listened quietly to my story across the desk, spoke a few sympathetic words, gave a scripture verse, a few words of exegesis, and said he'd like me to come back again.

I remember asking myself, *For what?* I did not return.

I knew of no mature Christian in whom I could confide. Even if I was of a mind to go for counseling, we had no money or insurance to pay for it, and I knew nothing about free services. Back then I'd never heard of support groups.

Such groups had proliferated by the time Caroline, whose story is told in Chapter 3, sought help. Several contributed to her recovery, including AL-ANON and secular groups for incest victims. Of one of the latter, Caroline says, "We had assignments in a book to do each week. The whole idea was to get the secret out. Sometimes that didn't happen until we wrote it down and read it aloud. The burden left when we spoke it to others." For Caroline, these groups were an important step in her healing.

Many Christians hesitate, thinking that they should not be seeking inner help from support groups that are not overtly Christian. A little information may help you decide.

Group Support

The modern support-group system began in 1935 when Bill Wilson and Dr. Bob Smith, themselves heavy alcohol users, saw the value of getting together regularly with people who had similar problems and working together to stay sober. The program came to be called Alcoholics Anonymous. In 1951, Dr. Smith's wife, Lois, founded AL-ANON for family members of alcoholics. The two organizations have become the father and mother of the modern support-group movement. AA's twelve steps have largely become their creed.

These days there are support groups for just about every problem known to women—from compulsive shopping to hot flashes. But the idea of receiving support in community with those who are like-minded predates AA's beginning in 1935. As a matter of fact, their principles are permeated with those of the Word of God.

Support groups build on the biblical premise that God means for us to live in relationship. The family was "Originally designed by God to be a nurturing womb," counseling pastor Melinda Fish reminds us. But she adds, "The modern-day family has for the most part developed unhealthy traditions."[1]

Besides, in our mobile society, families have been smashed and the shards scattered from Maine to California.

[1]Melinda Fish, *Adult Children and the Almighty* (N.Y.: Chosen Books, Fleming H. Revell Co., 1991), p. 23.

Members who remain nearby and are intact still may frown and shake their heads because they simply can't understand us.

It was God's original design that members of larger family units live in community and minister to others out of their particular strengths. To facilitate that, He instructed Israel to live in tribes, which were a form of extended family. Tribes as ancient support groups have existed in cultures throughout history.

Of course, God knew that because of sin's presence, no community system would work anywhere near perfectly, nor should we expect it to do so. Still, God, who is perfect, can minister to our damaged souls even through such imperfectness.

In western nations, tribal communities rarely exist. For a variety of reasons, we have separated from one another into nuclear units—and even those have broken down. As a result—and at a time when individuals are more damaged than ever because of the accelerated effects of sin in the human race—we find ourselves hurting in isolation. As a result, our pain is intensified. It's not hard to believe that a malignant force would prefer that we Christians live painful, lonely lives. The concept of support groups, where encouragement and love can happen, seems like the gift of God that it is.

The support group is one contemporary phenomenon that fills the gap left by our splintered culture. However, to a woman who is timid—at least in part because of past rejections—the doorway over which hangs a sign, "Support Group Meets Here," and her mental image of a roomful of staring strangers may be as attractive as a dark alley. The warning echoes: *I won't be accepted. I'll make a fool of myself.*

The picture in my mind of the evening I visited a support group with a friend is three-dimensional. *No pressure, a sense of realness, and a place to be.* The dozen or so who were present smiled their welcome, but they didn't come at me with prying questions. Those who spoke honestly expressed what was going on in their lives now. They were kindred, attached by invisible common struggles and victories and joys that warmed the stark room with acceptance and understanding.

Will *your* first experience be as positive? There are too many variables to make promises. But a support group definitely has the potential of being a place peopled with individuals who are striving for integrated lives and who will allow you to be yourself.

"It is exactly what the name implies—a place for a woman to gain support," states Lisa Call, coordinator of such groups in her church. If you need a human handhold and a kind of extended family while you're working through issues, it may very likely be for you.

Dr. Davis explains a second kind of group: "*A therapy group* is led by a professional and is usually a more confrontive and aggressive approach to attacking issues. In a support group everyone rallies around the person but doesn't necessarily confront or interpret a person's experiences. It's more like, 'We're all in this together. What can I do to encourage you to do better this week?' "

Therapy groups are held in places like counseling facilities, mental health centers, and women's shelters. "The leader focuses on his members in an in-depth manner. . . . He may use his individual counseling skills to help the member clarify and work through the problem. He can also use other members to play various roles. . . .

"We view the leader not as a counselor doing solely one-to-one therapy in the group but rather as an orchestrator who may focus on one individual for a period of time while involving other members in the therapeutic process."[2] You join

[2]Edward E. Jacobs, Riley L. Harvill, Robert L. Masson, *Group Counseling: Strategies and Skills* (Pacific Grove, Calif.: Brooks/Cole Publishing Co., 1988), p. 243.

such a group at the recommendation of a professional if he or she decides it is appropriate.

If you are considering a support group, you will need preparation. One way to do that, if your problems aren't severe, is to read some helpful Christian books on inner healing first. Lisa Call advises women who have experienced serious abuse to go to a counselor for therapy first since they may not be able to process the information they'll receive in a group setting. Whatever your situation, if God seems to be nudging you in the direction of a support group, take whatever steps He shows you are necessary to obey.

If your mind is packed to the walls with conflicting and confusing thoughts, and you can't sense God's guidance now regarding a group, talk with a mature Christian who can help you sort out ideas. *Don't give up until you find such a person.* Don't give in to the inner urge to slump into passivity. Keep remembering: Healing is a cooperative process. God guides you in specific steps, and you must take the initiative to act.

Support groups fall into two categories: secular and Christian. Let's look at each.

Secular Groups

Although some work through a particular book on inner healing or have their own format, the majority use AA's "Twelve Steps."[3] Members are expected to "work the program," which simply means to thoroughly apply a step to your own life, one at a time, until you assimilate that teaching. Various ways to do that are presented at meetings.

There is nothing mysterious or mystical about the steps. While they are man-made, they are not based on man's

---

[3]*Twelve Steps and Twelve Traditions* (N.Y.: Alcoholics Anonymous World Services, Inc., 1952), p. 42.

philosophy. Summed up, they say that I must admit that I can't fix myself and need God (called "a Power greater than ourselves") to do it, and I commit myself to Him for that purpose.[4]

After making (1) "a searching and fearless moral inventory," (2) I confess to God, myself, and one person what I've done wrong, making sure I'm ready for Him to remove my defects and ask Him to do so. (3) Then I make all the restitution I can, continue to search myself and admit when I do wrong, cultivate contact with God (as we understand Him), praying "only for knowledge of His will for us and the power to carry that out."[5]

Finally, as the result of our spiritual awakening, we share what we have learned and keep practicing these things ourselves. Keep in mind that it takes a lot longer to work through the steps than to read about them.

"We never have to do anything we are unable to do, truly find offensive, or don't want to do," says Melody Beattie of support groups. "When it is time to do or change a certain thing, we will know it is time and we will want to do it."[6]

Even though secular groups' describe deity *not* as Jehovah God or the Lord Jesus Christ but as "a Higher Power," some Christian women are comfortable with that. In their minds, they identify the "Higher Power" as Jehovah God, incarnated in Jesus Christ. These Christians are glad for the AA-type inclusiveness that allows a cross section of women to pursue wholeness.

Others, like my friend Katie, are uncomfortable with the vagueness of a "Higher Power." For that reason, she sought out a Christ-centered support group.

---

[4]Ibid.

[5]Ibid., p. 96.

[6]Melody Beattie, *Codependent No More* (N.Y.: Harper/Hazelden, 1987), p. 177.

Christian Groups

For Katie, a Christian twelve-step group felt much more like home. The emphasis was more clearly on Christ as sanctifier; the twelve steps had biblical comparisons. Although different groups adopt different biblical comparisons, here are some examples:

Step 1: "We admit we are powerless and that our lives have become unmanageable."

Biblical comparison: "I know that nothing good lives in me, that is, in my sinful nature. For I have the desire to do what is good but I cannot carry it out" (Romans 7:18).

Step 2: "We believe that we need to turn to God for help."

Biblical comparison: "He forgives all my sins and heals all my diseases, He redeems my life from the pit and crowns me with love and compassion" (Psalm 103:3–4).[7]

Both groups' formats are similarly informal. A secular, AA-style meeting will probably begin with everyone introducing himself or herself by giving a first name. Group members respond in chorus to each with, "Hi, _____." There may follow a minute of meditative silence and announcements. In a twelve-step group, the leader or a regular attender reads the steps and perhaps the Serenity Prayer as well. Someone will discuss one of the steps and ask volunteers to talk about their feelings and related recent experiences. An offering may be taken.

Groups that are studying a book will usually have a similar format but will discuss a chapter instead of a step. They may also do things like share in pairs on a theme, provide self-tests, or discuss a particular issue in small groups.

The format Lisa Call's Christian-oriented groups use is

[7]*Women in Recovery* (Salem, Oreg.: Trinity Covenant Church).

similar to many sponsored by other churches. It includes the singing of a few choruses, announcements, one person presenting one of the twelve steps from a Christian perspective and talking out of her life about that step. There is a brief devotional (in some groups a longer teaching). Commonly included is prayer time and small group discussions. Women who've been through the twelve-step program (and some repeat it) can move on to a group that is studying a book on codependency or another applicable subject.

Often a leader is someone whose own life has been fractured, as is true for leaders of secular groups. Cordie Pinner recalls her own beginning: "I had a whole lot of pain that I hadn't walked through adequately. Even though I'd had some counseling, I hadn't really gotten into the meat of that. I cried through the first two sessions. It took four or five times before I could talk out of my life. Nobody pressured me. We were given permission to talk when we felt as if we needed to.

"After I'd been through the Steps four or five times, the church needed group leaders. I realized that I needed to share the pain from my own life with people who have the same thing. So I took over a group."

Lisa Call says, "Probably half the women who come are very scared. The other half have reached rock bottom and are willing to try anything." Group leaders are not there to "fix it," but to facilitate this part of a woman's journey. As the women cooperate, God does the changing.

Some groups are separated according to particular problems: for example, sexual abuse victims in one and families of alcoholics in another. That's likely to be more helpful than having women with a variety of problems meeting in one group.

In some cases, a woman may be comfortable in a co-ed group. But in other cases—if she's experienced abuse, for example—she's better off with only females. Those who've been abused by men may be afraid of the opposite sex and will be hampered by the presence of men in such an intimate setting.

Not all who begin attending continue. Some women say, "It's just too painful. I'm not ready." It's a good idea for such a person to see a counselor, read books, attend a small group women's Bible study, go to a retreat, or talk with other women who are being healed themselves. When and if a support group becomes the right place for them, God, their Great Physician, will nudge them back.

Guidelines for Lisa Call's groups are typical of most—both secular and Christian. They include acceptance of others as they are and where they are; sharing; honesty; active listening; refraining from criticizing, preaching or giving advice; keeping confidences; remaining silent when one wishes; praying for one another; allowing others time to speak; and commitment to attendance and to one's own healing.

"We talk about the fact that this process hurts, but that's the way healing comes," Lisa says. "We're not there to give Sunday smiles and keep going. Yes, the Lord is there and He loves us so much that we'll never understand it. But life hurts so much we can hardly stand it, too. Those things coexist all the time. We have to be real about both parts.

"I tell them that they are hurting right now, but the Lord is their rock and strength. We all have to lean on Him every day. He redeems our life from the pit and crowns us with love and compassion. *But Lord, it hurts.*

"We never shame our women. We must create a trustworthy environment for them—make sure that the group is a safe place. As necessary, we go back over the guidelines to insure that safety."

"Trust grows slowly," Cordie adds, "as women begin to share their stories with one another."

The Fruit of Healing

Lisa and Cordie both agree: "Healing is a slow but life-changing process. Those who attend begin to return to the churches they've left because of anger, lack of trust, or the ability to believe that God loves them. That's one of the most incredible things. What happens isn't just emotional healing—it's spiritual healing as well."

I've met women for whom a support group has proven to be one important step in the re-formation process. It's one of the places that shaping and polishing take place. The process is much like that of Pueblo Indian potter Margaret Tafoya who shapes her clay "Coil by coil, into strong graceful forms." Her finished pieces deserve places of honor.

"The secret," she says, "is in the polishing." Part of the ancient process she employs is to shine a vessel's surface with stones. "Her polishing stones—family heirlooms passed down from mother to daughter—are more precious to her than gemstones. 'I value them like my heart.' "[8]

How much do you value your heart? Enough to let God polish it anew, using others as His polishing stones to make you shine?

Thinking It Over

1. Have you had preconceived ideas about support groups? What new insights do you have?
2. In what ways can a support group fill the gap that once may have been met by extended family?
3. Which of the following would be your priorities in choosing a group?

---

[8]Marjorie Hunt and Boris Weintraub, "Masters of Traditional Arts," *National Geographic* (January 1992), p. 82.

- meets in a nice room
- is Christian-oriented
- has an experienced leader
- is made up of people I know
- practices confidentiality

4. If you're not aware of the AA and Christian support groups available in your area, consult your phone directory, public library, and large churches to get that information to have for reference.
5. Check the statements that apply to you:

_____I feel alone in my problem.

_____I wish I could learn how others are working through their problem.

_____I need to make myself accountable to someone.

_____I get discouraged in the process and need encouraging.

Evaluate your responses. Do they imply that you need to look for a support group? Ask God for insight.

6

The Healing Word of God

One thing I knew very soon after I was converted to faith in Jesus Christ: The Bible was God's Word and could change my life. That's why, as my eldest son, John, rode his trike up and down the sidewalk in front of our apartment house and his younger brother, Paul, napped in his carriage, I sat on the steps and read my Bible. I was as full of holy awe as a pilgrim to Gethsemane.

My wonder was kindled by a sense of the presence of the Spirit of the Book—and also the memory of my mother rocking and reading it for wisdom and comfort. As I sat on the stone step, I heard her speak from yesterday. *"Marion, this Book is the only thing I have to leave you. But it's the most important thing I own."*

At first, the Book's unfamiliarity made me frown. But gradually understanding came. Each insight was like a caress from God. "You are born again. Now you can understand my words. I am speaking to you from its pages."

Several years later, however, when I picked up the Book to read and reflect, I felt as though it was mostly accusatory. Now my painful, lonely childhood had caught up with me. Even though I was a "full-time Christian worker," I felt as overwhelmed as I had when I was a child caring for Mama during her frequent serious illnesses.

In childhood, it had been: *Be sure to put her medicine where she can reach it. Soup on the burner by her bed for lunch. The bedpan empty and at her bedside.* As an adult it was: *Be serene and radiant, the way a grown-up Christian lady and pastor's wife should be.* I was sinking further, beneath a weight.

The Weight of Perfectionism

Damaged people tend to superimpose their perfectionism on Scripture, supposing that's what God is requiring of them. I was doing that, and the result was to feel more inadequate and guilty. The words in the Book, once as delightful as *A Child's Garden of Verses* when I was eight, now seemed dark and ominous in my hand. *You are not measuring up.* For one thing, although the Spirit of the Book still lived in me, my soul was panting so loudly from its struggle to keep face that I could scarcely hear the still small voice.

But the Bible was life. So I'd settle my new son, Mark, in his crib for a nap and collect the Book and settle on the sofa. I'd press myself: *Let the Word of God transform you.* But no internal miracle seemed to be taking place. Choking on disappointment when the time was over, I'd get my hands into something that produced quick results—folding laundry or putting away dishes.

I could relate to a woman who told me recently, while her psyche still vibrated with aftershocks: "Most of the time when I read the Bible, it triggers guilty feelings." I'd recovered from the same painful disease—seeing the Bible more as accusation than promise. More a lecture to a perpetually disobedient child than a call to come home to Love.

After all, doesn't the New Testament say, "If anyone is in Christ, he is a new creation; the old has gone, the new has come" (2 Corinthians 5:17)? Doesn't that mean we should be grown-up Christian ladies now, with our "God-makeover" complete?

Doesn't the New Testament also say, "Put off your old self"? *Like a set of clothes? Ones that we rip off and toss in the trash?* "Put on the new self." *Redrape ourselves with the Jesus nature? In an instant, while the clock strikes seven?* (Ephesians 4:22–24).

No matter how hard we concentrate and pray, we can't make it happen.

Something's wrong with me!

So it is not surprising that damaged women I have talked with generally agree: Of all the means God has provided for their healing, it's Scripture that they use least often.

Marie and the "Sword"

Marie's experiences show how that can happen—how we can turn away from the Word when it becomes too painful. I met her as I traveled to another part of the country to conduct a seminar. She recalled, "My mother died when I was five and my grandmother came to live with us. She didn't like me and instructed my dad to discipline me quite harshly and made sure that he did it.

"I was raised with fear and superstition—ours was not a Christian home. I was told I was bad and I believed it. Now I realize that I was a child of the shadows, lonely and a spectator.

"When I was eleven, my grandmother took to her bed, and that summer I was in charge. That meant getting breakfast at five A.M. for Dad, packing lunch and supper for him, waiting on my grandmother and a younger sister. I carried water, heated it on a coal stove, did the laundry and carried the water out when I was done. I chopped kindling and carried in firewood, canned garden produce, churned butter. Childhood was never fun.

"At seventeen, I ran away and married into a church family that was dysfunctional. I discovered that my husband was an alcoholic. My children were raised in the church from the first Sunday. We looked like a normal family, only because we kept our secrets well hidden.

"One night my husband threatened to shoot me in front of our five children. The youngest was eighteen months. I couldn't take any more of the abuse and was afraid he'd kill all of us, so I left and got a divorce." Marie kept her children.

"Somehow, I believed that the things that happened must have been my fault. Through a long period of my life, I'd find myself asking, 'What's wrong with me?' "

What distorted thinking patterns might someone like Marie superimpose on Scripture? What wrong ideas might she read into it?

God couldn't possibly want me close to Him. He couldn't possibly care about me. I'm an outsider. I don't belong. I'm bad. Passages that describe Him that way don't apply to me personally. I only deserve punishment. God is someone to be afraid of the way I was afraid of my grandmother and my father and my husband. My job in life is to take care of people and to work hard. But I can't do and be everything God expects of me. I'm guilty . . . guilty . . . guilty.

Pain and shame can blind us and cause us to wrongly interpret God's Word. That's what I did when I read 2 Corinthians 5:17 and Ephesians 4:22–24. My mind had jumped to perfectionistic conclusions instead of absorbing the truth.

Paul was *not* telling believers that they should experience a Hollywood-like transformation. "The old (previous moral and spiritual condition) has passed away. Behold, the fresh *and* new has come!" (2 Corinthians 5:17, AMP). He *was* telling them that they had been given a new godly nature and the *potential* to live out of it because of God's empowering grace.

Likewise, in Ephesians 4:22–24, Paul is summing up a similar Christian principle: We changed positions at our new birth. From being a child of Satan, we became a child of God. As a result, we are to choose to "be constantly renewed in the spirit of your mind—having a fresh mental and spiritual attitude" (AMP).

Reclaiming God's Word

Some Christians are uncomfortable with support groups, healing seminars, and "all this grace talk." They fear that it pulls people away from the full Word of God, favoring a few positive-sounding promise verses.

On the contrary.

Reclaiming the whole Word of God comes with healing. First, a woman comes to see the particular experiences and wrong perceptions that have influenced her. Next, she does what God shows her so that the past loses its hold. Gradually, that woman's vision adjusts.

Our thought processes can be compared to a plot of earth in the southern United States on which had been planted the notorious kudzu, originally introduced to promote soil conservation. Stubborn, tenacious and hardy, kudzu proceeded to root and spread until it choked out natural flora.

Controlling kudzu is no simple, overnight process. Neither is changing so that we see what Scripture *says* clearly and not what we *think* it says. But it can happen because the Holy Spirit who inspired the Book is also our present Counselor.

Here are specific ways of thinking that may be causing you to misperceive the Word of God. Along with them are new ways of thinking to straighten out your mental kinks and twists.

Old way of thinking: *I'm inadequate. I need to keep proving my worth.*

New way of thinking: *I'm valuable to the God of the universe; accepted and loved by Him. His Word says so. My worth is determined not by man's view of me but by God's view.*

After the Holy Spirit first began to reveal my identity to me through a female Bible teacher, a passage like Psalm 139 became a balm instead of an abrasive. Before, "O Lord, you have searched me . . . and have known me" (v. 1) would have made me fearful and guilty. *God is watching me.* Now, the words reassure and make me confident. *God is here caring for me.*

Old way of thinking for the woman who was sexually abused: *I'm bad. I'm guilty.*

New way of thinking: *I was violated, taken advantage of. I am not guilty. I have not broken God's Word.*

Old way of interpreting a passage as simple and straightforward as Philippians 4:6, "Do not be anxious about anything, but in everything, by prayer and petition, with thanksgiving, present your requests to God": *But I am anxious—all the time. I can't stop. So God won't answer my prayers.*

New way of thinking: *It's because God knows I'm anxious that He invites me to continually surrender my anxieties to Him. This passage is not an accusation. It intimates that God understands; it's an invitation.*

Words of Life

To use the Bible in the process of healing, read passages that are simple and direct and nonthreatening at first. Later, you'll be able to read more challenging passages. My recommondation to the woman who said she could open anywhere in the Bible and feel guilty was to read only Ephesians 1:1–14 for two weeks. There, Paul describes our biblical identity—not as inferior and rejected but as blessed and chosen and adopted and loved and sealed.

A Christian counselor I know recommends clients read one or more of the Gospels and list all the names of Christ and see who He really is.

If you chose the gospel of John, for example, the first name would be "Word." Since "Word" means that Christ is an expression of God, you'd reflect on the fact that Jesus is actually God in a human body come to earth. The Father is no longer remote but knowable.

If the idea of God as Father scares you to death the way it does many women because their human fathers were abusive and unloving, begin reflecting (not merely saying the words) on the Lord's Prayer. Do so frequently and prayerfully before God. In this classic model, Christ identifies Him as our Father. Let this new, true image of Him soak into your spirit.

What kind of Father is He? Here's what the Lord's Prayer implies: He is one who is absolutely worthy to be worshiped; His will is perfect and can be completely trusted; He'll provide our needs; He'll forgive our sins and enable us to cope with temptation and the Tempter.

God sometimes calls specific passages to our attention during times of pain, and means for us to cling to them. They become our private treasure. When I was on my knees crying my ache to Him, Jeremiah 33:3 became one such treasure: "Call to me and I will answer you and tell you great and unsearchable things you do not know."

"What things, Lord?" I prayed.

Wait and see.

"Do you promise?"

I promise.

A promise that my friend Fran clung to included Peter's words: "And the God of all grace, who called you to his eternal glory in Christ, after you have suffered a little while, will himself restore you and make you strong, firm and steadfast" (1 Peter 5:10).

One of the most freeing actions we can take is to become a true student of Scripture so we'll personally discover its true meaning. The New Testament, for example, was written in a Greek that is very precise in the meanings of words for a reason: We can know clearly and distinctly what God wants us to know.

A good practice is to look up key words in an English dictionary, a dictionary of Bible words or a word study book, an exhaustive concordance like *Strong's* or other translations of the Bible. By doing so, we'll discover precise meanings for ourselves. These books are available in many libraries and Christian bookstores.

One subject that seems to have confused many of us at one time or another is *anger*. When I've asked women's groups, "Do you think that it's sinful to be angry?" some answer almost in chorus: "Yes!"

With that mind-set, it's easy to suppose that "in your anger do not sin; do not let the sun go down while you are still angry" means that anger is sinful (Ephesians 4:26). But that's not what it says.

The first word translated *anger* is an "abiding, settled attitude of righteous indignation against sin and sinful things." "And sin not" is provided as a check and a restraint. The second word translated *anger* is accompanied by "irritation, exasperation, embitterment."[1]

So, after research, we learn that anger can begin righteously but escalate to a full, rolling boil and a passionate

---

[1] Kenneth S. Wuest, *Wuest's Word Studies in the Greek New Testament, Vol. I* (Grand Rapids, Mich.: Wm. B. Eerdmans Publishing Co., 1973), pp. 113–114.

urge to get even. On further reflection, we realize that *becoming* angry is not a sin. It is part of our God-given emotional makeup.

We're warned, though, that there is a difference between righteous and unrighteous anger. Also, we are not to allow that to escalate until it pushes us to the point of spouting abusive language. We're to deal with the anger. Admit it to ourselves; confess it to God; ventilate our feelings; ask for God's grace to forgive; choose to count on His provision moment by moment; take constructive action regarding the event that angered us in the first place.

A second subject to study, because it gnaws at the fiber of damaged women's souls, is *guilt*. Much of our guilt is false, however, and at first we're unable to distinguish which guilt is legitimate and designed to prompt confession so we can receive forgiveness, and which guilt we wrongly heap on ourselves.

Our Firm Foundation

Two wonderful passages can lead us out of the condemning woods. The first is Romans 3:23–24, which states that all of us have sinned but that we are all also declared guiltless by grace through Christ.

Here, we may get stuck by self-condemnation unless we define sin correctly as to "miss the mark" or failure to obey the law. Only then is guilt legitimate; it is not when it comes from the paralyzing tyranny of a wrongly programmed conscience. I meet many women who cannot tell the difference between the two and feel condemned by much of what they read and hear. They need help from a mature Christian to learn true discernment.

Always remember: We are accepted by God in the same way a child is accepted by a loving parent. Because of her love, that parent chastens when necessary so the child will grow into a healthy adult. The purpose is not to tear down but to build up. That is the foundation of truth we stand on when we are in Christ.

The second passage, 1 John 1:8–10, should prompt a deep sigh of relief. We *all* miss the mark. Every human— even the one you've put on a pedestal—is a sinner. There are no other kinds of people.

Forgiveness for legitimate sin is *always* available. Reflect on verse 9 often, emphasizing key words: "If we *confess* our sins, he is *faithful* and *just* and will *forgive* us our sins and *purify* us from *all unrighteousness.*"

Faith is a third subject to which we need to give our attention. Our trust in God may have been eroded because we've supposed He couldn't be trusted. *Didn't He allow these things to happen?* That thought may be a dirge that resounds repeatedly in our mind. So it is vital to see how and why we can trust Him.

As we've already seen, man's inhumanity to man grows out of our common sinful nature. God abhors sin and the wounds it causes, and He clearly says so. But, due to our self-centeredness, we humans act out of lust, not love. That's not God's fault. It's ours. He's given us a free will and will not rescind it.

The Scripture keeps reaffirming the fact that faith is *a choice to trust God* because of who He is described to be. To see biblical trust pictorialized read Genesis 12:1–7, the drama in which God said to Abram, "Leave your country . . . and go to the land I will show you." He had no road map with the way highlighted and the destination distinctly identified. He was simply asked to trust God. "So Abram left, as the Lord had told him" (v. 4).

We grow faith; it is not given us full-grown. Look for ways in which the Bible teaches that. For instance, we "*grow* in the grace and knowledge of our Lord and Savior Jesus Christ" (2 Peter 3:18). No Miracle-Gro here.

We grow it little by little by internalizing the truth from Scripture about who God is. Choose to act on what you know. Ask God to provide grace or wisdom or guidance for a particular need on Tuesday or Friday, then notice how He's actually done what you asked for.

Isolate the truths about God in passages like the following and reflect continually on them:

> Because of the Lord's great love we are not consumed, for his compassions never fail. (Lamentations 3:22)
>
> I will sing of the Lord's great love forever; with my mouth I will make your faithfulness known through all generations. (Psalm 105:8)
>
> You then, my son, be strong in the grace that is in Christ Jesus. (2 Timothy 2:1)

It may seem imperceptible, but down deep, faith is taking root.

A fourth topic urgent to every woman's recovery is *love.* Even though I'd taught about God's love to every age group in the church, I couldn't believe He loved me. My subconscious insisted *God loves the world as a whole, not you personally.*

For months at the beginning of healing, I reflected on passages recommended to me, and now the Holy Spirit was applying them to my spirit. If you ask Him, He'll do that for you too. Ephesians 1:1–14, already mentioned in this chapter, was one such passage. So was Psalm 139.

The apostle John's gasp of wonder was a third passage: "See what [an incredible] quality of love the Father has given (shown, bestowed on) us, that we should [be permitted to] be named *and* called *and* counted the children of God! And so we are!" (1 John 3:1, AMP).

As you reflect on these four subjects—anger, guilt, faith, love—and others, count on the Holy Spirit to illuminate His truth and shine it into your spirit so the words become an absolute by which you live.

Besides our private time with God, He renews us through His Word at group Bible studies or Christian support groups.

Angie, whose story is told in Chapter 4, listened to Charles Swindoll's *Insight for Living* weekday mornings on her way to work. "I couldn't have made it without the radio. I wasn't being fed at church, and for family reasons I couldn't go elsewhere. I have no doubt that God led me to listen. I wasn't able to use all I heard, but it gave me insight into what life could be like."

Reflecting regularly on Scripture during our healing process so that we cultivate a strong spirit becomes the warp and woof of our daily lives. We are being made new in the attitude of our minds (Ephesians 4:23). "The renewal here is basically an act of God's Spirit powerfully influencing man's spirit, his mental attitude, or state of mind."[2]

As we finger the fabric of Truth, then slowly wrap ourselves in it, we will find places in our soul being healed. *"Be transformed by the renewal of your mind. . . .* This passage is talking about a renovation."[3]

That renovation is thorough, but gradual—a section at a time, the way a couple across the street from our home restored their house. First, they removed the roof and built the attic into a second floor. Next, they removed the front and built a closed-in porch. After that, they ripped out the downstairs walls and made a dining room and then a larger living room. But they accomplished it a board and a nail at a time.

---

[2]H. Norman Wright, *The Christian's Use of Emotional Power* (N.J.: Fleming H. Revell Co., 1974), p. 39.
[3]Ibid., p. 40.

Thinking It Over

1. Respond to the statement, "Most of the time when I read the Bible, I feel guilty."
2. Review "old ways of thinking" from this chapter. Write your thoughts about ones with which you most identify. Then reflect on "new ways of thinking." Which ideas do you need to keep prayerfully reviewing so they'll become part of your thinking?
3. Read Ephesians 1:1–14 every day for a week. Underline verbs that tell what God has done for you. Put your name in the verses.
4. Summarize main points about one of the following subjects: anger, guilt, faith. Journal your questions and struggles. Pinpoint actions you need to take, and ask God to help you do so.
5. When you hear the words "God loves you!" what do you think? How has a parent's attitude colored your view of God's love? If you think that preconceptions about His love are coloring the way you see it in the Bible, ask Him to reveal those preconceptions to you.

7

Open Up in Prayer

"Prayer kept me from losing my mind."

The reason for Marie's turmoil was that she'd been sexually abused by an older male relative on five occasions when she was just entering puberty. "I told my mother and she was sympathetic, understanding, and horrified. When she told my father, he said to me, 'I hope you're not making this up, because God will punish you if you are.' My dad owed this abusive relative some money and now refused to pay it. Many times, I felt as if my dad sold me for that owed money.

"I hated myself. I just knew God didn't love me anymore and I was going to go to hell. Eventually I became abusive to myself. On one occasion, I remember scratching my arms with a scouring pad until they bled. By now, I hated everything and everybody.

"Thank God for prayer. I have been a pray-er since way before the abuse. Even when I was sure God didn't like me and I was on my way to hell and stopped going to church for years—I always prayed. Isn't that ironic?"

She prayed even when, as a very young teenager, she began to abuse children herself and blamed the Holy Spirit for her lack of control. So many others have found themselves in the same miserable, painful place.

Of all the gifts given mankind, the ability to know and dialogue with God with its potential to salve and solve is the most breathtaking. When our souls are on "empty," we probably pray hardest. And yet, because our minds are darkened with pain and guilt, we feel little benefit—even though we know intellectually that God has given us the gift of prayer to be a wonderful lifeline.

No One Else to Go To

Perhaps like Marie, we continue to pray even when we are convinced that we are too sinful for God to care about, or feel that He has betrayed us. After all, where else can we go? Or perhaps we're afraid *not* to pray. For although we may think that God is at fault for our misery, we worry that He could allow things to get even worse if we don't bow in contrition.

Praying was what kept me able to function when I was grieving over losses and shivering from insecurities. Beside my bed, on my knees. Walking city blocks, talking silently with God. At three in the morning again on my knees.

If we are daughters of God because of our faith in Jesus our Savior, even at our worst moments we can be assured that the expression of our needs are incense before the throne. "The Spirit helps us in our weakness. We do not know what we ought to pray, but the Spirit himself intercedes for us with groans that words cannot express. And he who searches our hearts knows the mind of the Spirit, because the Spirit intercedes for the saints in accordance with God's will" (Romans 8:26–27).

We live in a broken world, the apostle points out in Romans 8, *one that is waiting to be liberated.* While we wait, we already have the Holy Spirit living in us. Kenneth Wuest explains that the Spirit of God lends a helping hand when we don't know how to pray—and He does that all during our spiritual recovery. Mary used the same word for "help" when she complained to Jesus about Martha. "Tell her to help me"—or, "Tell her to lend me a hand."

The Holy Spirit doesn't take over the responsibility for us, giving us automatic deliverance without any effort on our part, Wuest points out. The Greek word for *makes intercession* " is a picturesque word of rescue by one who happens on . . . one who is in trouble and 'in his behalf' . . . 'pleads with unuttered groanings.' "[1] During that emergency process, He prays *in* us because although we don't know what to ask for, He does.

On an ordinary morning in midlife, the Holy Spirit who lives in me heard my own weeping spirit as my hands did morning chores. He graciously interceded, finally drawing out of me a prayer that, at the time, I didn't fully understand. "God, help me. I don't know who I am!"

The Holy Spirit has come to us to take our problems as His burdens. He prays for us. He prays for us with "groans that words cannot express, because the Holy Spirit doesn't use human speech. His prayers for us are spiritual breathings from His deep concern for us."[2]

While the Spirit does pray for us, God also wants us to tell Him our thoughts and feelings. I refused to do that most of the time because I was ashamed.

Even if we do tell friends, family, counselors, and support groups, none is a replacement for telling God. He is never distracted and is the perfect listener. Besides, He has all power to get to the heart of our situation.

---

[1]Kenneth S. Wuest, *Wuest's Word Studies in the Greek New Testament* (Grand Rapids, Mich.: Wm. B. Eerdmans Publishing Co., 1973). p. 141.
[2]Maurice R. Irvin, "The Intercession of the Holy Spirit," *Alliance Witness*, 7–20–83, p. 22.

Can we really dare tell God our Father about obsessive thoughts and anxieties? The most commended people in the Bible were the ones who were honest with God about their humanity—and that included their feelings. They can set the example for us.

David was unrelenting in the way he expressed himself to God. "I am worn out from my groaning; all night long I flood my bed with weeping and drench my couch with tears. My eyes grow weakened with sorrow" (Psalm 6:6–7a). Because David did, I began timidly to show the Father my own feelings. "See how scared and depressed I am?"

Some days when I seemed to have no prayer words of my own, I came to see that I could pray a Psalm. That was one reason God included them in the Bible. I could put them in my own words and tell them to Him. Try doing that with all or part of Psalms 8, 13, 22, 25, 31, 38, 43, 63, 86, and 139.

Wordless Praying

On other days when I was too full of grief to talk with God, I realized I could just sit in His presence and feel my feelings before Him. Just as I can communicate wordlessly with my husband, so also I can communicate wordlessly with God. That also is a kind of prayer.

Another reason we feel as though we can't pray is that our minds are so fragmented with bits and pieces of mental debris. When that happens, I urge women to tell God every thought fragment. After they do, their minds will be more free and they can talk coherently with Him. "I feel so guilty about this. . . . Show me if it's real or false guilt." "I feel so lonely. . . . Help me to know if the reason I don't have intimate relationships is my fault."

If you think that . . .

Christians shouldn't feel depressed or angry, so you'd better keep quiet or just confess your feelings as sin . . .

Remember . . . Christians are human. We *do* feel like this. Feelings are not sin. They are normal human responses. They *can* lead to sin if we don't express them and get help.

If you think that . . .

God won't help because you can't get on top of things long enough to pray the way you imagine you should, or you've repeated the same requests to Him so long you're sick of them and are sure God must be too . . .

Remember . . . God's expectations for you at this stage in your life are very likely not as lofty as your own. If you're a Christian, when He looks at you He sees the perfection of His Son—which has been imputed to you—not your moral inconsistencies. Instead of grimacing and turning away, He hugs you to himself and walks with you through the recovery process in an infinitely patient manner no matter how much you fail.

Be His child. Start your conversation right where you are. Say whatever's on your mind. Keep sidling closer; ask the Holy Spirit to help.

Hearing His Voice

But who wants to talk to a God who never talks back? During my painful years, God seemed taciturn—stonelike, impenetrable, and unresponsive.

What I came to see was that God *is* a communicator. He invented communication, and from the time He walked with Adam and Eve, He's been doing so. At stone altars, on Mt. Sinai, in the wilderness, in the tabernacle and temples, through angels, through the incarnation of His Son, and through His Spirit. Remove the "God saids" from the Bible and we'd have an emaciated volume.

So why do some of us have such a difficult time hearing Him? I believe my own experience is typical: I was too noisy inside to hear. That was also true of a friend, as evidenced by her conversation with her counselor.

"What's your goal for me?"

"To help you become quiet enough to hear God."

She and I both had to learn to rest.

Able to Hear Correction

Another reason we don't "hear" God is that since His is a silent *spiritual* voice and not an audible one, we must cultivate our God-given spiritual sense in order to do so. That is exactly what we do during recovery—silence the sounds of guilt and fear and slow down from our frantic need to prove our worth so we feel free to take time to listen and cultivate our spiritual dimension. The more we practice the disciplines of healing and center on the Spirit of Christ within and follow Him, the more acute our spiritual hearing will become.

"Ninety percent of my healing came through prayer," Julie told me. "Everything was precipitated by the fact that I poured out my need to God."

From a family of seven children, Julie and two of her sisters were sexually abused by their father. "I remember when I was three years old, I knew that something wasn't right. Looking back, I realize that there was a lot of inappropriate touching until I was eleven and the sexual abuse got worse." Julie describes her father as a very kind man—"so kind he didn't have much backbone. He didn't abuse maliciously but because he was addicted to doing so.

"I had a nurturing mom who says she wasn't aware of what was going on. I think she didn't want to believe it. She made sure we had a close family system, but it was very dependent. When I fell apart after I met a man I really liked and later was called on the carpet at work for not following through with my responsibilities—I knew that something was wrong with me."

Julie read books, attended seminars, and had counseling. "I saw God as a father I could trust despite the role model my biological father set, probably because my mother was so nurturing and she was a father image. So I was able to move into prayer as a healing place. My mental image of being in prayer is with the angels behind me and me at God's feet, usually with my head on His lap.

"I learned to trust God enough to let Him tell me what I *needed* to hear, not just what I *wanted* to hear. Prayer isn't just one-way—it's two-way. It wasn't enough to *tell* my heavenly Father; healing came when I allowed Him to tell me. I had to get past the initial grieving and crying out and say, 'Okay, God, what do you want to do in my life? I'm open'—and really mean it, not just go by rote.

"He really did answer. He showed me places in me that were unhealthy. Sometimes I didn't want to hear it, and I shed many tears as a result. But then He'd let me know, 'It's okay. It hurts, but I'm showing you a part of you that I want to change.'

"I was accountable now that God had showed me. That meant continuing on and not shutting God off—*See you later.* Trusting Him enough to go back for more. Not for punishment, but to trust Him enough that if He's going to tell me what's wrong, He'll also bring change and healing."

A New Accountability

Whenever we show God a raw spot, it is like showing a slash or gouge to our medical doctor. He may not prescribe for us what we expect, but then, he is the doctor and we are not. Whatever way the Eternal Physician answers is right for us now. *Wait, something else has to happen first.* Or as with Julie: *Take a look here at your unhealthy behavior. Do what I show you.*

A "get-going" attitude toward God is one of the most futile and draining we can have. Through prayer, Julie was not calling God into action to sprinkle her with fairy-tale magic so she would shazam from scullery maid to princess. We won't either. But prayer will set the process of healing in motion. Honest, cooperative prayer like Julie's keeps us on track.

Forgiveness, one of the most vital aspects of prayer to women like us, is also one of the most misunderstood. The guilt-plagued woman is discussed in Chapter 6. If she has done something that is genuinely wrong and confessed it, then she's forgiven and made clean (1 John 1:9).

If she has genuinely accepted God's forgiveness and cleansing and not argued against it in her mind, she knows she is forgiven. However, she may have to speak the truth— *I am forgiven*—to her disbelieving self many times during the process. If she's still feeling guilty, the guilt she feels is probably false, and she needs help to deal with the whole issue.

True Change

Some women suppose that repentance means they must beat themselves emotionally. A woman needs to ask herself: "Is that the trap I've fallen into?" Keep in mind also that repentance means to change one's *thinking* about the issue in question. It does *not* mean that one's behavior will automatically or instantly be changed. Sometimes we need to work in order to "produce fruit in keeping with repentance."

God does mean for us to change our behavior. But as we

have seen—like so many other things in the Christian life—this will likely be a process that *follows* repentance. Right behavior grows out of right thinking, and the God who lives in you is the One who, by His *grace,* enables you to steadily align your thinking and your doing.

Another prayer that may seem to go unanswered is to be able to forgive those who have injured us. How does a forty-year-old woman forgive the man who began sexually abusing her when she was three? How does a thirty-five-year-old woman who still has a hard time knowing what she thinks forgive the person who never allowed her to think for herself?

Perhaps we are praying wrongly, expecting forgiveness to descend like a golden gift from heaven. Like faith, forgiveness is both a choice and a process. "I think I have forgiven my uncle because I have chosen to do so. But the memory of what happened keeps returning to my mind. Does that mean I haven't really forgiven?"

It does not. By choosing to forgive, a woman has taken the only step she can. *I give up my desire to get even. Punishment is your job, Lord, not mine. I understand that the other person is a sinner just like I am. Giving up my hatred and my desire to punish doesn't mean that society shouldn't place a penalty on the perpetrator because he broke the law.*

Should a woman expect to forget what happened to her? Hardly. "Please keep in mind that in Bible terminology, 'to forget' does not mean 'to fail to remember.' "[3] Because we are humans and are so created, we do remember.

Warren Wiersbe also points out that in the Bible " 'to forget' means 'no longer to be influenced by or affected by.' . . . *It simply means that we break the power of the past by living for the future.*" That's what Joseph did with his brothers who'd mistreated him. "Joseph knew that God had . . . a

---

[3]Warren W. Wiersbe, *The Bible Exposition Commentary* (Wheaton, Ill.: Victor Books, 1989), p. 89.

race for him to run, and in fulfilling that plan and looking ahead, he broke the power of the past."[4] When Paul said he was forgetting things behind, he meant that he "refused to be controlled or absorbed by his past heritage or attainments."[5]

The more we pray for God's grace to operate in our lives, the more our anger will subside and the more readily a sense of forgiveness will settle in. "My grace is sufficient for you," Christ said. "For my power is made perfect in weakness" (2 Corinthians 12:9).

Because of God's inworking, the event will not be called to mind instantly and with passion at every triggering. For God is healing that memory with the salve of His love and is providing the ability to see others involved from His perspective.

Should we be praying for reconciliation with the perpetrator? Of course. But we may have to leave that step with the Lord because other things have to take place before that prayer can be answered. "I feel guilty sometimes because I am not willing to be reconciled with my father. But he has not changed. He has not repented. He is the same corrupt, destructive individual he always was."

This woman needn't feel guilty, because reconciliation isn't possible at this time. She can get past old anger and resentment, but because her father is unchanged, she cannot be united with him the way she'd like. Neither can she trust him at this point, for he has not owned up to the wrongness of his abuse.

We can be reconciled to another only if he or she is repentant. Even then doing so is a process; for faith, like a bridge, must be built a section at a time.

---

[4]Ibid., p. 90.
[5]Waalford and Zuck, *The Bible Knowledge Commentary* (Wheaton, Ill.: Victor Books, 1983), p. 661.

Not only does God heal us through private prayer, He does so through prayer with others. Over the years, I've approached women to whom God has directed me to be a prayer partner. Each of them was someone with whom I felt mutuality and rapport. We'd meet weekly, discuss needs, and pray for each other. When schedules changed and caused us to not be able to meet anymore, I'd eventually ask God to direct me to someone else.

Ask the person who has come alongside you to hear and help, to pray with you. On days when your soul begins to crumble, call an understanding friend who's been with you during your journey and ask her to pray with you.

Commitment to Prayer

You may want to find a small Bible study group for women where attendees pray together and keep confidences. Healing prayer is part of many support group sessions. Leader Cordie closes each session by calling members into a circle. "We pray together holding hands. There's something about joining hands that helps the bonding. Then we hug around the circle. Before we did that, women didn't bond as quickly or as deeply."

Keep talking with God—when your insides ache, when you're sorrowing, when you're empty, when you feel hopeful, and when you have no hope. Say whatever is inside to God and listen. The more you communicate, the more knowing will grow. And out of knowing—that most intimate of all relationships—healing comes.

Thinking It Over

1. Of all the kinds of prayer you can think of, which do you pray most often? Which do you enjoy most? Least? Why?

2. Think of times prayer has made you able to function when you were grieving over losses and shivering from insecurities. How did it do that?

3. If you're uncomfortable telling God about your negative feelings, what reassurance do you find in Psalm 6:6–7a? In Romans 8:26–27, when you can't seem to put in words to God what you want to say?

4. If you're frustrated because you aren't hearing from God, is it because of the way you've been taught? Because you're too noisy inside? Or because you expect to hear an audible voice? Are you unfamiliar with your spiritual dimension, that inner life where God communicates to Christians? Where do you need your divine Counselor to take you from here?

5. If you've been having trouble forgiving someone, is it because you haven't made a choice to do so? Do you suppose that forgiveness means that the ugly incident and its misery will never again take a front seat in your mind? Do you suppose you shouldn't have angry feelings toward the person? Do you expect that the two of you should automatically be reconciled? Rethink the subject and journal your conclusions. Tell God that you're counting on His grace working in you to be completely healed from the anger.

8

Worship: Touching Hearts

The hour when I felt forsaken
I heard the Spirit whisper,
"God is,"
And chose to go on.
Learning to trust
Through each pain came.
Finally I stood
And haltingly took a step.
The world out my window
Began to come alive.
Faith cried:
"See God's mark?"
I worship.
In my spirit
I know Him.
I am home.

Something yanks me out of sleep. A dream? A noise? I
burrow more deeply beneath the covers, hoping that, warm
and secure, I'll drowse and drift off.

Instead, my mind is standing at attention, picking through the dark, ugly corners of yesterdays. *How could He . . . why didn't I . . . so lonely . . . how long. . . .* Silently, I slide out of bed and kneel on the cold floor to beg and pray. The emptiness has come over me again.

Silence from heaven. Feeling even more alone, I sob soundlessly into the mattress, making a wet place. Why doesn't God touch me with His love? Why do I listen and wait in the cold darkness, and hear and feel and sense nothing but the raging of my insides?

My knees hurt and I'm cold, so I slip back into bed feeling as stiff and chilled inside as I do out. As I lie with eyes closed, I am startled by the words of a chorus singing in my mind. They say things I do not feel: *"hallelujah . . ."* and *"joy. . . ."*

I choose to pick up the refrain and sing the words to God, and as I do *hallelujah* and *joy* take root in my spirit. When I finish that chorus, I think of another and choose to sing it in my mind; and when it is through, I find myself praising God for bed and quilt and this holy moment.

The Shift

What has happened? The Holy Spirit has prompted me to shift my focus from *myself* and my *problems* to refocus on the Father. Inevitably for all of us, that shift must take place. This also is part of God's way of healing.

Will He always woo us to worship Him every time we need to do so? He will not. He'll open the window to personal worship and show its loveliness. Then He'll call us to choose daily. Will we drop our pleading for help and appreciate Him simply for who He is? This, too, is a hard thing to learn: to seek the Healer instead of shouting and flailing about the wound.

At times, you may sense God shifting your gaze. He may show you a flower in a yard, or alert you to the sound of geese migrating overhead, and you are distracted like a child by a soft or shiny thing. For moments you forget, and when you remember again, your inner gaze has been gently turned from yourself.

Mostly, worship is furthest from our minds as it was from Job's. Hear his words as he sat on the ash heap. "I cry out to you, O God, but you do not answer" (Job 30:20). At the end of the discourses, God reminded him of why he could praise: "Where were you when I laid the earth's foundation? . . . Have you ever given orders to the morning, or shown the dawn its place?" (38:4, 12). Job bowed in awe.

Worship is the place to which the apostle John was drawn one Lord's Day while he was imprisoned on Patmos.

David, who often began a psalm with the lament "Why, O Lord, do you stand far off?" often ended with praise. "The Lord is King for ever and ever" (Psalm 10:1, 16). *You are the all-loving, all-powerful King of the Universe and I simply worship you.*

A. W. Tozer, whose writings have mentored me, says that "God made us to be worshipers. . . . He created man out of . . . an internal necessity. . . . God had to have some creature that was capable of admiring Him and loving Him and knowing Him."[1] Therefore, in worship, we fulfill our purpose. Be assured that God is a waiting participant and not One who needs to be coaxed away from running the universe.

Take Time

Learn to create times of worship. W. Phillip Keller, who felt insecure and caged in his urban environment, had to

---

[1]A. W. Tozer, *Worship, The Missing Jewel of the Evangelical Church* (Harrisburg, Pa.: Christian Publications, Inc.), p. 7.

choose to "search for some still waters."[2] Doing so took single-minded determination for Keller and his wife, Cheri, as they turned a rural cottage into their place *to be.*

Still Waters became home, and the Kellers were quietly awed by the wonder of their place. "Swallows . . . calling cheerfully to their newly fledged broods . . . orioles . . . in search of insects drowsy with dampness."[3]

So will our place of worship become home and a place of wonder. That's because, during these times, we experience relationship unencumbered. Only two together. Though our questions have not been answered nor the holes in our souls mended, this moment we know joy in our spirits.

The definition of worship is to reverence or honor God. Since our concept of the Lord is unique, as are our feelings and our place along the journey, the way we hallelujah Him will be just as unique. What will be right for you during dark days? Here are bold suggestions in the Pslams from which to choose.

Sing to God. In your mind or at the top of your lungs, melodiously or not so. To the radio, to a tape, to your own accompaniment (Psalm 33:1–2).

Play instruments. For the psalmist it was on a ten-stringed lyre and harp. For us, if we're musically proficient, it may be on piano or guitar. If not, we can make music to his name with tambourine (Psalm 92:1–3).

Clap . . . and shout. God is awesome and a great king, so He deserves our full expression (Psalm 47:1). During a hike in the back country or at home with the cat watching. Not because we *feel* like it, but because we *choose.*

Dance. "Let Israel rejoice in their Maker. . . . Let them praise his name with dancing" (Psalm 149:3). One of my

---

[2]W. Phillip Keller, *Still Waters* (Berkhamsted, Herts, England: Word Publishing, 1985), p. 14.
[3]Ibid., p. 56.

most retiring friends, who has been on a healing journey, says, "When I'm alone, I love to turn on music and dance around the living room before God."

Quieter ways to edge into the light . . .

Bow and kneel. Often a position of worship creates an attitude of worship. But if this physical position isn't possible for you, do so in your heart (Psalm 95:6).

Speak words to God. Keep remembering that you may have to do so through an act of your will even though your feelings are A.W.O.L., simply by remembering and reflecting to Him the implications of some of His names. *Shepherd. Rock. Love. Lord* (Psalm 145:3–6).

"*Be still* and know that I am God" (Psalm 46:10). Be humble before Him in your spirit, a creature in wordless worship. Drop your defensive thoughts and blaming, and allow Him to show you where anger or self-pity comes from in you.

Sabbath Rest

Before we can worship with anything that resembles consistency, we may need to rest, because we are too churned up within even to think seriously about focusing wholly on God.

That was true of me. It was then that God taught me about relaxation and rest through a book to which He had led me. Reluctantly and guiltily, I'd saunter to a chair and let my body relax completely, experiencing seconds of inner stillness.

After I was physically at ease, I learned to focus my mind on the presence of God. *Lord. You are here—this moment—in me.* I was at worship. Anyone can learn to relax, but only Christians can rest wholeheartedly in the presence of God.

Paradoxically, it takes persistence. The Word tells us to

"labor" to get into God's rest (Hebrews 4:11a).

I learned that I could rest in the presence of God anytime. So I chose to be still before Him and unite with Him and relate the task in hand to Him. As I peeled potatoes. As I raked the yard. For seconds only at first; then for minutes. Once a woman learns to focus on God even briefly, the joy of it will motivate her to practice that way of living even more.

With a new awareness, I saw and heard my world and was drawn to praise for birds on a feeder and last roses of summer. Out from within, there grew an "awakening." I realized that I could worship anywhere, anytime. I imagined young David, tending sheep under the stars and praising Jehovah in the silence, and I felt akin. The greatest of wonders filled me—that I could live in the painful kingdom of this world but still be at home in the kingdom of God.

Worship took root and sprouted as a way to be any time during any day. A whole place to live. Standing in front of a pet shop window talking to a fuzzy, yapping puppy straight from the hand of God. While eating that wonder of wonders—a banana. Seeing the sun after days of Oregon gray.

From the Wells of Your Soul

The things that will call you to kiss God's hand differ. For one friend it is children. "I love to be with them; they draw me out of myself." Without planning it, she finds herself worshiping her Father.

For another it is recalling a rocky cove, wind lashing and ocean roaring around her. The image of safety in that cove draws her to worship God as her shelter in the storm, and to be there with Him.

To women who are beginners, I recommend a look at the natural world. A tree out the window. The favorite dog lying at your feet. Flowers arranged in a vase on the table. Or pictures like the ones I have deliberately collected and put in an album: a bee on a dandelion; a butterfly on a marigold; a sunset.

More often than not, it is God's creation that moves us from ourselves to Him. "Light. I know not a single word fine enough for Light . . . holy, beamless, bodiless, inaudible floods of Light. . . . Go to Nature's school—the one true University."[4]

Private reverence has been called meditative prayer, for worship and communion meld like waters becoming a body. The steps, Richard Foster advises, are "centering down" or "re-collecting of yourself. . . ." Precisely because the Lord is present with us, we can relax and let go of everything, for in His presence nothing really matters, nothing is of importance except attending to Him.

"The second step . . . is 'beholding the Lord. . . . ' I mean the inward steady gaze of the heart upon the divine Center. . . . Worship and adoration, praise and thanksgiving well up from the inner sanctuary of the soul." The third step is to listen to God.[5]

One of the elements of worship that helped me immeasurably if I was scraping bottom was to give thanks "in all circumstances" (1 Thessalonians 5:18). It didn't take place, though, until a serious dilemma was resolved.

I had to know: Was I being asked to thank God "*for* all circumstances"? No. I was not asked to proclaim, "Hallelujah, I have been mistreated and maligned." But "Thank you, Lord, for being able to turn this miserable circumstance into an opportunity to show something about yourself."

On really bad days, I actually brought before God every

---

[4]Tom Melham, *John Muir's Wild America* (Washington, D.C.: Special Publication Division, National Geographic Society, 1976), p. 22.

[5]Richard Foster, "The Celebration of Meditative Prayer," *Christianity Today* (Dec. 7, 1983), pp. 22–25.

item I could think of for which I could be thankful. A phone call from a son. Pictures in the mail of grandchildren. Blossoms on a plant that until now had seemed doomed for the compost pile.

The War of Doubt

I have to confess. I was a skeptic of such simplistic, Pollyanna-like exercises. But I was proven wrong. Giving thanks this way was certainly not all there was to making my way upward, but it was a significant part.

Mini-retreats are also a good weapon in the war on darkness and doubt that seeks to shut out God's light.

Years ago, a writer friend described the times she'd take a folding chair, Bible, and pen and drive to her favorite spot by a stream. There, she'd be with God for an hour or two or three in worship and reflection. Another friend said that she went into her bedroom for the same purpose when no one was home.

I had no favorite stream nearby. There was a park with a bench or, in cold weather, a second-floor table and chair by a window in the public library where I could see trees and squirrels.

Whatever the place, distractions have to be minimal, for we are easily pulled away. As we re-collect and grow quiet inside by resting and focusing on God's presence, we worship and reflect and dialogue and feel pain and praise and sense God's holiness and repent and worship again.

When words fail, we can, as with prayer, use God's own. "My soul praises the Lord and my spirit rejoices in God my Savior. . . ." "Praise be to the God and Father of our Lord Jesus Christ, who has blessed us in the heavenly realms with every spiritual blessing in Christ . . ." (Luke 1:47; Ephesians 1:3). "Hallelujah! For our Lord God Almighty reigns" (Revelations 19:6). We'll find our spirit taking up the theme.

Joining With the Body of Christ

We are not solitary worshipers feeling our way around in space for God. If we are believers, we are temples wherever we go. His very Spirit lives in us. We are holy temples because Christ's righteousness has been imputed to us. "Let us then approach the throne of grace with confidence" (Hebrews 4:16).

When temples join together in worship, all heaven can break loose. The affirmation that results when pews full of fellow believers hold God high can assuage our feelings of abandonment and aloneness. *I am not a solitary soul struggling to hold on to God by my fingernails. I am part of a body that is Christ on earth. I am joined invisibly to these sisters and brothers. Here together in this place we are knowing Him. Joined consciously in communal purpose with Him. Fulfilling our highest calling. We have eternal meaning.*

God wants to use corporate worship as part of your healing. So no matter what's happened before, don't isolate yourself from the body of Christ now. Enter the sanctuary with a resolve to worship from your heart. *I come here to praise with my spiritual family.* Our role models are the Israelites coming together with a psalm on their lips: "Lift up your hands in the sanctuary and praise the Lord" (Psalm 134:2). Behind those lines we can almost hear a gasp of anticipation.

Perhaps you enter your church thirsty for Him—only to leave just as parched because the worship seemed flat and uninspired. You want choruses and they sing hymns, or vice versa. They use only organ accompaniment and you want guitar and drums.

Because we are different, the kind of congregational worship that kindles us will vary. Ideally, we are most comfortable with people who are like-minded. If corporate worship seems dull, you may want to visit other churches, with other worship styles, to see where you best fit. Or attend interchurch women's meetings where the music and praise draws you to God and other women. But if that's not an option, keep in mind that there is hardly a traditional Christian hymn through which we cannot laud and honor God if we sing from mind and heart.

Fear of embarrassing yourself may prevent you from wholehearted corporate worship the way it did me. When the music started so did my tears. *I must remain in control*, I insisted. At first, I waited for "heads bowed, eyes closed" to wipe my eyes. Finally, I began to accept the fact that crying for me at this stage was normal and probably healthy.

Tears still come from time to time during worship in church. If I'm the only one doing so as far as I can see, I don't mind. Emotions were created by God, and tears when I am moved is one way to express them to Him. These days, though, I weep not so much for myself as for the knowledge that I have apprehended the beauty of the Lord. As a matter of fact, to be so moved I count a privilege.

You may need to tiptoe timidly into the place of worship. What you'll find is that doing so is as natural to your spirit as breathing is to your lungs. In community with spiritual family, you sense an extendedness of yourselves. United before God with others, you get a glimpse of what wholeness feels like.

From Doubt to Trust

In the end, worship is a movement: from self-centeredness to God-centeredness; from doubt to trust. You will find yourself trusting God more when you have been consciously in His presence. Doing so does restore your soul and builds your faith.

That is especially important if you have been feeling toward God the way the goldfish in a picture a friend gave me must feel toward the cat leaning into the fishbowl. Tongue out, the feline's paw is ready for the catch. The picture's caption is: "Trust me."

Doubt and anxiety may be so powerful that it is oppressive. But despite our feelings we *choose* to count on what we know intellectually: *God is love. God wants my worship.* Even so, all we may *feel* are the aftershocks of trauma and not a sense of His presence. Nevertheless, we *choose* to wait, to listen, to speak, and to sing.

By faith we have let go of our internal ache.

By faith we perceive God as He is described in Scripture, not as we have wrongly imagined Him.

By faith we speak words of praise.

At first a trickle, then a rivulet. Finally a stream of living water bubbles from within.

" 'Come to me. . . .' The people came. They came out of the cul-de-sacs and office complexes of their day . . . and He gave them, not religion, not doctrine, not systems, but rest.

"My prayer is that you, too, will find rest."[6]

Worship God.

Thinking It Over

1. Are you comfortable worshiping God privately or do you need to cultivate that ability? Why is it a good idea for you to do so when you're unhappy? What sacrifices will you have to make?

2. Choose a way to worship mentioned in Chapter 8. No

---

[6]Max Lucado, *Six Hours One Friday* (Portland, Oreg.: Multnomah, 1989), p. 32.

matter what your mood, do so each day for several days. Keep a record of results. What conclusions do you draw?

3. Now experiment with new ways to worship. Which ones are most effective in taking you out of yourself and your problems?

4. What scenes or events create in you a desire to worship? Become aware of these during the day and take time to act on them. Also, either make a list of things for which you can be thankful or take a mini-retreat in enjoyable surroundings.

5. Go to church and let the melody and lyrics penetrate your soul. Let yourself feel part of the body. Show God your thoughts and feelings and invite Him to fill your spirit as He did the Old Testament temple.

9

Discover Yourself Through Journaling

Edward Robb Ellis began keeping a journal on December 27, 1927 (he was sixteen years old), because he'd challenged some friends to see who could keep one the longest. Ellis won by a landslide: From that day, he never stopped writing. His collection became so voluminous that it threatened to crowd him out of his apartment, so he donated it to the Archives of Contemporary History at the University of Wyoming at Laramie where he attended college.

Keeping his "diary," as he calls it, "is a daily confrontation with one's unconscious . . . and I'm always discovering things about myself."[1]

Sue Monk Kidd calls journaling "an excursion into my heart . . . journaling helps ground me in a quiet center. . . . It offers me a way to touch my deeper, contemplative self—the 'Mary' side of the Mary-Martha duo."[2]

I cannot agree heartily enough. Like other women with unsteady souls, I had a strong need to tell, and journaling

[1]Herb Kram, "Diarist Who's in a Class by Himself," *Grit* (Feb. 19–25, 1989), p. 2.
[2]Sue Monk Kidd, "Making Visible the Sacred Tale," *Virtue* (July/Aug. 1991), p. 36.

was a nonthreatening way to do so. Writing my thoughts has proven to be one of my most therapeutic activities. Much different from the diary I kept while growing up—which was mostly an account of where I went and what I did—in this I write from my insides.

A Book of Remembrance

My initial reason for journaling, twenty years ago, was that established professional authors often kept journals. The day of my resolve, I fished a green plastic loose-leaf binder out of the wastebasket dumped there by a gleeful son on the last day of school. A would-be writer, I saw this as my launching. Later that day, I began:

"I don't know what I'm supposed to write in a journal, but here goes."

At first, it *was* more of a diary. "Paul had a test in Government and got one of the three top grades in his class."

"Car radiator leaking. Through a friend, we were able to get it welded for only $10."

Gradually, though, I began writing down things that bothered me. The day I had to make a bank deposit for an organization of which I was treasurer, I admitted to my journal: "I'm worried because I always seem to get the paper work wrong. Prayed for help." The next day I added, "Did everything right!"

My friend Rebecca began keeping her journal when she went into therapy. "I had a hard time verbalizing, so my counselor suggested it. Writing my thoughts and feelings allowed me to discover and examine them. It was such a relief. These were things I wanted to say out loud. I needed that sense of communication. I'd never had someone to listen to me before. Besides, things that we say out loud get lost in the air. Writing is solid. Thoughts and feelings are preserved."

Those who are highly vocal and whose need to tell is very strong are sometimes reluctant to give up their much-speaking in favor of writing. But eventually they realize that even our most devoted listener cannot always *hear* us any more than we can always hear them. At that point, journaling becomes an attractive option.

When I speak to women's groups on the subject, I can almost hear some thinking back to me: "I don't have time." "I don't like to write—period." So I quickly point out that we can put down as much or as little as we choose—even a few lines.

Some women draw pictures that re-create an experience or memory. A sketch depicting: *Me sitting at the table trying to eat dinner when I was about nine. Dad argumentative and Mom frightened. I stare down at my plate. My stomach is tied in a knot. I want to be excused. They want me to stay.*

You may journal in a way other than pen in a notebook. Rose uses her computer. She began journaling at the same time she began learning to use that machine, so it was a natural melding. Another possibility is to talk into a pocket-sized tape recorder.

"But I'm undisciplined. Spontaneous," a woman told me yesterday. Fine. For now, keep a notebook handy and jot a few lines spontaneously about an experience, a mood, a response to a conversation. Estelle jots thoughts in a small notebook she carries when she takes long walks. That's her "thinking time." Besides, writing that way is less intimidating for now than the formal process of "journaling."

Find your personal style. Be ready to change that style of journaling as you change. Above all, don't let journaling become a legalistic ritual.

Learning to Be Free Within

"For some people, learning to be free in their diaries is a way of learning to be free with themselves."[3] If you're using a notebook, the kind may either enable or restrain you. When I wrote in a reclaimed loose-leaf, I felt less restrained than the months that I used a prettily bound volume with a segment for each day. Find one that allows you to write most freely.

Keep reminding yourself that a journal entry is not a homework assignment, so you can't do it wrong. Misspelled words, wrong sentence construction don't matter. Neither do you have to organize your thoughts. "Sometimes I start with one thing and then switch to something else and then go back to the first subject again," Rose admits.

Another objection women have is that *someone may read what I've written.* "I hide my journal," women admit in my workshops. Others tell family members that they're private so please do not read them. Those journaling on computer may be able to use a password, and unless an individual knows that password, he or she cannot open the file. The conclusion that most of us finally reach, though, is this: *No one is interested in reading our journals.*

Another question that stymies some is: To whom will I write? It may be to the journal itself. One of the first, soaring discoveries that Rebecca and I made was that through this practice, we had actually created a listener. Not that the book took on a life of its own; but by getting our thoughts outside our heads, we ourselves had become the listener. *I hear what I am thinking and feeling.*

At other times, you may write directly to God or to any of the individuals who have peopled your lives. "My son has a disease and I write letters I won't send to physicians who've

[3]Tristine Rainer, "The New Diary—Where Anything Goes," *Writer's Yearbook,* 1979, p. 57.

made me feel very frustrated," a friend said. "I even write speeches and include a description of what I'd wear if I were to deliver them." Several other women I help have written letters in their private books to individuals who have abused them.

"Telling my uncle on paper how I felt about his victimization of me was one of the most healing things I've done," a woman who had been in therapy for years told me. It was a turning point for her.

Sharing what you've written with a Christian helper may extend the benefit. Since journaling was part of her therapy, Rebecca dropped her week's outpourings at the counselor's office beforehand so he'd be ready to discuss it during her appointment.

"I wrote for myself, but it was also a way of communicating with him." Another counselor I know encourages clients to do the same thing. "If they don't feel free to share certain parts of their writing, I ask them to photocopy what they do want to let me see and bring it in."

New Light

A second discovery I made was that God counsels us through our journaling. Just as He can guide our thoughts during prayer, He can also provide insight as we write. *Of course! The Re-creator is part of everything I do, and that includes this.* Even though we may not realize it, each day that we journal, we do so in His presence.

The *reason* I sometimes sensed an inner door opening as I wrote about yesterday was because God was enlightening the eyes of my heart in order that I might know the hope to which He has called me (Ephesians 1:18). Every time you pick up your pen, count on the fact that God really uses journaling to help you become intimate with yourself. Don't let His presence intimidate you; instead, count on Him to hear what you write and to draw you into all truth.

Some of the ways He does that:

He encourages you to write your grief in words of passion. He coaxes you as gently as the parent of a toddler learning to walk: *Release in your private book feelings over deep, wrenching losses and brutal kicks to the heart. Ashamed/ useless/ bitter/ boiling/ uncertain/ uptight/ afraid/ aching/ torn/ confused.*

God knew I needed His gentle urging because I was frightened by my feelings and ashamed of them. Rebecca, on the other hand, needed no coaxing in this area. "If I'm really mad, I put down how I feel and why. It's never bothered me to do that."

As for me, I finally understood that when my feelings rose like floodwaters near our former home and I needed a concrete way to "verbalize," I could write those passions down, reflect on them and see them in God's light. In the beginning, I tore up my writings.

He urges you to empty your mind on paper. One way to do that is to tell Him your thoughts in prayer. A second way is to journal those bits and pieces as they hop around in your brain. Writing them nails them securely. *Trespassers apprehended.*

He enables you to gain insight when you reflect over experiences. In the seventies, I wrote: "Today, I crossed the street rather than to have to run into Harry. I was afraid he wouldn't remember me and I thought that if I spoke first, he might just look blank. Then I'd feel humiliated. I'm ashamed, Lord. Change me."

He helps you discover patterns in the way you think, feel, and behave. Avoiding people like Harry, I discovered from journal entries, was a behavioral pattern because I felt inferior and insecure. God redeemed me from it by revealing *His* acceptance of me and love for me.

A New Sense of Personhood

Gradually, I learned to walk down the avenue feeling secure. I still wanted the Harrys and Janes and Susans to respond warmly, but if they only gave a perfunctory nod or none at all, my self-worth wasn't shattered.

Patterns you may uncover include avoiding relationships or being too eager to establish them; shunning all confrontation or behaving too antagonistically; losing your temper or seething silently in resentment; demanding too much of yourself and others or living haphazardly and goalessly.

Over the years, God gave me insight into a myriad of behaviors and provided grace for change, as He will do for you. One yearning was a strong need to be who I am. Early in my journey I wrote about wanting freedom:

"Freedom . . . to be alive in my own special way. Freedom from having to do and to feel successful today. To sit and think.

"I want to be totally absorbed in the moment. Right now I see starlings and a blue jay fighting for bread Mark scattered on the grass. Tiny sparrows wait in the trees. When the bigger birds have gone, the smaller ones pick up the tiny remnants. I want the freedom to take time to reflect on that."

Later:

"I want to be real . . . to be me. A woman who loves color; who feels like yelling or being quiet . . . who sometimes tends to eat when she's not hungry to fill another kind of need. One who is not Peter or Paul or David (although they were human too), but is herself."

Other facets of my life the process brought to light:

- PMS was a factor in the way I felt.
- I was a person who internalized the days' tugs-of-war and needed to change that.
- Although I had faith for some things, I was terribly afraid

of being without money and needed to learn to trust God for my material safekeeping.

To trace these patterns, we must reread what we've written every few weeks or months. Often I do that during mini-retreats. "I hate rereading," an inveterate journaler told me. "It's embarrassing to realize that I thought and felt that way."

I understand. It's done that to me, too. Especially when I see how often I've repeated myself:

"So tired tonight. Felt pressured to finish a manuscript and still work in the yard."

"Stressed out from today's schedule. And part of me sees that things still need to be done."

"My son commented that I always seemed to be working. I couldn't forget his words."

A tendency to overdo? Definitely, Lord. I see it here. Driven. Do only what you give me time and strength for? I see, Lord. Keep helping me to change.

When Sue Monk Kidd developed stress-related chest pains she wrote, "I unfolded the experience in my journal. . . . I saw the perfectionist who dwelled in me, arrayed in all her pomp and glory. . . . I unearthed this truth in my journal. It became one of the biggest turning points in my life."[4]

Contradictions

We'll find that we also contradict ourselves. "I hate Bill. He's impossible and being around him makes me cringe."

"Part of me cares about him. I wish we could be close."

"He slices me with his words. There's nothing between us and can never be."

---

[4]Sue Monk Kidd, "Making Visible the Sacred Tale," *Virtue* (July/Aug. 1991), p. 36.

"Probably it's my fault, at least in part."

Repetitions and contradictions are part of growth. We must see a thing repeatedly and variedly until the truth becomes part of us. We think and feel this way today and that way tomorrow because we're humans in process. Through God, out of ambiguity will come single-mindedness.

Accept the self you describe in your journal. Write from inside yourself without censoring your words and accept that as the person you are right now. Because you are a living human being, your thoughts and feelings will change; that's normal. Seeing dispassionately who and how you are now enables you to gain perspective. Invite God, your Creator and Re-creator, to change you in His way and time—and cooperate with Him.

"Bring to your rereading an assumption—the assumption that God was present when you made your entries and that therefore you can confidently look for His presence in the movement of your life."[5]

Keeping It Fresh

To keep from growing stale, try some of the following exercises. God can energize them and, as a result, take you down roads you might otherwise have missed:

- Keep a personal history with God the way the author of Psalm 136 did for the nation of Israel, writing one-line stanzas and repeating the refrain. We, like they, need to *know* what God has done for *us*. Instead of a vague "Yeah, God has answered prayer" in our personal history, we cite specifics that become a platform for faith. A beginning of mine might be:

[5]Roland R. Reece, "Discover Yourself," *Virtue* (Jan./Feb. 1987), p. 29.

"Who enabled me to speak with power at a retreat even though I had been injured,"
His love endures forever.
"Who allowed me to visit my sons scattered across the U.S. this year,"
His love endures forever.

- Write things you hate to do, can't wait to do, and dream about doing. Describe what makes you happy and sad; angry and worshipful; and what these reveal about yourself.
- Have conversations with your conscience when it's been insisting you are guilty, guilty, guilty.
- Write expressions of thanks to people in your past and present who have been helpful in some way, whom you may have taken for granted.
- Ask questions. "Why did that situation make me so angry?" "What's going on here?" "Why do I feel this way?" "What am I learning about myself?" "How does that apply here?"
- Identify times when you feel most frightened. Most safe. What conclusions do you draw?

It is not enough to write about ourselves in relationship to our environment so we see who we are. That can easily discourage us. *I am undisciplined. Moody. Self-occupied.*

We need also to reflect in our writings on God's Word so that we'll grow confident of His help in our sore places and internalize what kind of women He will help us become. *"May the God of peace himself make you entirely pure and devoted to God; and may your spirit and soul and body be kept strong and blameless until that day when our Lord Jesus Christ comes back again. God, who called you to become his child, will do all this for you, just as he promised"* (1 Thessalonians 5:23–24, TLB).

Journaling her feelings helped Angie (whose story is told in Chapter 4) admit that she was angry about her life. But it was meditating on Scripture and writing what she saw that made the difference. "I spent almost a year studying and journaling through Isaiah. I put down my thoughts about each section as well as cross-references I looked up. It was wonderful.

"Isaiah 61 talked about restoration. 'I delight greatly in the Lord; my soul rejoices in my God. For he has clothed me with garments of salvation and arrayed me in a robe of righteousness, as a bridegroom adorns his head like a priest, and as a bride adorns herself with her jewels.' (v. 10). It started coming to me that restoration comes from God, but I have to put it on. He's not going to pound it into me.

"Not one thing in my circumstances has changed. I am the one who has changed." As a result of what Angie was learning from God, she "had to let go of a lot of things. That was the answer."

At retreats, when I ask for a show of hands of women who have journaled, many say, "I used to but I haven't for quite a while." I, too, have had months when I don't write a word.

Reasons vary. Life may be pretty ordinary and there seems to be little to write about. Then internal tension draws us back. "I've begun journaling after a long time away," a friend told me over lunch recently, "because I'm going through some hard stuff."

Another friend avoided her journal for months, she now realizes, because she was angry and unwilling to work through the reasons and make the necessary surrenders. When she finally did begin again, it helped her move forward.

A Life "Companion"

So, although journaling may be cyclical, once we discover its healing properties, we will count on it as a significant other or even a life companion. But not even a journal should *replace* dialogue with real, live humans. As a listening place, though, it will always be there for us—helping us open up, enabling us to see afresh—preparing us to talk with others when opportunities arise.

For novices or veterans who haven't touched a journal in a long time, the best advice I've ever heard on how to get started is this: "Write fast, write everything . . . write from your feelings, write from your body, accept whatever comes."[6] No fanfare, no gritting of teeth.

So it will have maximum value, let's follow our biblical leaders—the psalmists. They described it all:

Their misery: "My bones are in agony. My soul is in anguish" (6:2–3).

Their isolation: "Why, O Lord, do you stand far off?" (10:1).

Their rejection: "How long, O Lord? Will you forget me forever?" (13:1).

Their hopelessness: "How long must I wrestle with my thoughts?" (13:2).

And through it all . . .

Their hope: "I am still confident of this: I will see the goodness of the Lord" (27:13).

They did. I can, too.

Where's my pen?

Thinking It Over

1. Journaling can be a healing activity. Which of the following needs do you have that it might help meet? A

---

[6]Tristine Rainer, "The New Diary—Where Anything Goes," *Writer's Yearbook*, 1979, p. 58.

quiet center? For self-knowledge? Tell my thoughts? Gain perspective over my problems? What do you conclude?

2. If journaling is new to you, get started by taking the following advice: "Write fast, write everything . . . write from your feelings, write from your body."[7] If you haven't been consistent at journaling, experiment with one or more of the following: a new kind of notebook; a new time to journal; a new way to journal; drawing pictures; writing to God, to another person, to yourself.

3. Is there someone to whom you need to write a letter that you won't mail? If so, do it now.

4. On separate days, begin writing by reaching deep inside and completing one of these sentences.
   Today I feel . . .
   I keep thinking that . . .
   An experience that keeps coming to mind is . . .
   What I long for most is . . .
   Something that keeps haunting me is . . .

5. Ask the Counselor to enable you to make enlightened discoveries as you read His Word. After you reflect over a portion, journal your response beginning like this: "(Your name), here is what God is showing me. . . ."

---

[7]Ibid.

10

The Church as Family

The little dog crept along in the shadows, coming into an open place only when he detected no human around. Even then, he was as alert as a combat soldier, one ear trained for the slightest sound. Debbie spotted the canine down the street and tried to coax him close with food, but his fear outweighed his enormous hunger.

So she left the food out for him to eat when he felt safe. Soon he crept forward, and she slowly, painstakingly sidled near until she could finally touch him. Beneath the stray's long, matted fur she felt only bones. The pads of his feet had been burned, apparently by some human degenerate.

Debbie desperately wanted to keep him, but she had too many pets already. So she hauled the dog to the Humane Society, expecting him to be adopted by someone who ached for him as badly as she did.

When Debbie returned home, a neighbor told her the distressing news that the dog's chances of being adopted were very slim. "The fact is, they'll probably have no choice but to put him to sleep."

To sleep? You mean, kill him?

Debbie grabbed her car keys and ran out the door, already

hugging the dog to her in her mind. *He has to be nursed and nurtured and loved.* At the Humane Society, she wrote out a check to pay the required fees for the stray and took him home.

A vet confirmed that Toby, as he came to be named, had been badly abused. But with care the dog filled out and his coat took on luster. Everywhere Debbie went, Toby followed. When she left the house and he couldn't accompany her, Toby waited by the door until she returned.

From a once terrified, skitterish stray, he grew into a trusting, friendly pet. After Debbie became my daughter-in-law when she married my son Mark, Toby became *my* friend. From the first, he expected to be accepted by me. *Your house is my house. Right?* From the first, he jumped on my lap and settled down. *Here's where I belong.*

The Fear of Church

Often when I scratch the ear that stands up and the ear that doesn't, I rethink the "Toby Story" and marvel over its similarity to my own and those of women I know. Like him, we've come begging the bread of acceptance and belonging—not in a neighborhood backyard, but at the local church—terribly frightened that we'll be rejected instead of fed.

Like Toby, some of us have been burned. So ambivalence tears at us. *The church is a haven. A healing place,* hope insists. The wounded part of us objects. *Church is judgmental. Demanding. A closed corporation. Unseeing and uncaring.*

The problem may not be in the church, but in us. Until I admitted "something's wrong with me," Christians couldn't soothe my painful places. For years I hadn't even admitted those areas existed. Now I was needy and knew it, but no one inside the sanctuary must know. After all, I'd been a leader in churches for years: I did not dare to reveal my true self before the saints. Instead, I pretended to be the same old me even though it was a lie. Walking down the aisle, I felt like A. J. Cronin's hero in *The Keys of the Kingdom*: "The oddity, the misfit, the little crooked man."[1]

Other women, however, do suspect churches—and for good reason. "When I was empty and hurting, I attended a church but instead of ministering to me, people condemned me. The leaders said if I were doing things right, I'd be okay."

"Our church simply refused to face the fact that any of us could have wounds. Those problems simply didn't exist as far as they were concerned." In these cases, the problem was in the churches.

"Dysfunctional," David Mains says of them. "Certain people . . . could be members of two dysfunctional families—their individual family and the family of God."[2]

For still others, the problem is an individual within a particular church. "This woman was very verbal and destructively confrontive. After she got done with me, I wanted only to get away and never come back."

Another complication we face is that when we're in pain, we tend to draw away from intimacy, like the bristlecone pine which, when trouble comes, pulls inside its trunk. We probably shrink back from any slight or frown the way Toby did from any noise. What he needed most, he was reluctant to pursue.

Just as Toby's avoidance of Debbie was self-defeating, so is spiritual amputation from the church, for *whatever* reason.

---

[1] A. J. Cronin, *The Keys of the Kingdom* (Boston, Mass.: Little, Brown and Co., 1941), p. 149.
[2] David Mains, *Healing the Dysfunctional Church Family* (Wheaton, Ill.: Victor Books, 1992), p. 9.

For Christ's body provides hands to console; shoulders to lean on.

The *Whole* Body of Christ

Keep in mind that there are *two* churches: the invisible, living body of Christ on earth threaded throughout the world, and the local assemblies. A woman becomes a member of Christ's spiritual body the moment she receives Him into her life. In that one, she is always accepted by the Living Head.

In any given local assembly, though, not everyone will necessarily welcome us unreservedly. Keep in mind that every member of "First Church" may not be a member of the body of Christ at all. No matter how many years they've been on the rolls, they may not be born from above.

If you are already comfortable in a local Christian church where you feel accepted no matter how you are, humbly thank God for the healing He is doing and will do through it. If you're not, begin to search for one, not merely as a place to experience corporate worship, but because such a place is meant to be family and is part of God's healing for you.

Even in a near-perfect church you may not be embraced and drawn in instantly. Expect to go slowly the way Debbie did with Toby. Take into account your expectation of rebuff. Here's one woman's account of her experience:

"I went to this church week after week and waited for someone to ask me what was wrong and to offer comfort. No one did. I recognize now that I was expecting them to read my mind and know something was wrong. It took all the strength I had to follow God's leading and gradually take the initiative in making acquaintances myself instead of waiting for others to do that."

Adjusting Your Heart

No, you should not settle for abusive legalism or an over-controlling leadership. But you may also need to adjust your heart when it comes to settling into a local body of believers. "Love the *real* and not the *ideal*," I once heard a pastor say in a sermon about the Church. *The real is flawed*; imperfect here, it will be transformed into the Bride of Christ there.

Think of local churches as family groups—each with a particular lifestyle and purpose for being. Look on the bulletin board or in the church bulletin for their statement of purpose. That will tell something about their mission. Listen for the heartbeat of the assembly instead of judging it by the insincerity of the greeter's smile, or the coolness of your pew mate. The greeter may have a migraine, and the worshiper next to you may be as needy as you are.

After you're seated and settled and singing, look slowly around at the congregation. One voice. One spirit. Strangers perhaps—but family, sounding the name of the Lord.

Focus on otherness. Those who are ill and being prayed for. Missionaries learning strange languages in strange cultures. Pay prayerful attention to what's being said and taught, expecting the Spirit to have a word for you.

Recognize your tendency to impose your mind-set on people around you. *They won't want to know me.* Choose to operate out of truth instead. *God himself accepts me and created me a wonder. He's living in me now. I am already part of Christ's body. I can take the initiative and move toward these others.*

Move from the larger family gathering where you are corporate participants seated in rows, to a smaller gathering where you participate individually. Where you can know and be known. It may be a women's Bible study, a prayer cell, a care group, shepherding group, etc.

If you begin to feel dissatisfied because your local assembly is faltering in "family-ness," ask yourself: Am I attempting to stuff members into my mold, wondering why they just won't fit?

Members are different from us and from one another as well. No two of us are mirror images. Ann is bubbly and loves small talk; Dee is quiet and serious. Ann distracts me from myself; Dee listens and gives insight. It's our very differentness that enables us to fill in the gap for one another.

A Place to Be Real

On the other hand, we will not be helped—and we may be hindered—if the church is not a safe place to heal. How does one recognize a church that is not safe?

David Mains suggests that such churches parallel the traits of broken families. They are perfectionistic and "don't allow for mistakes . . . pretend no one in the church has a problem with greed, or lust, or a nasty tongue, or manipulation, or alcohol."[3] So naturally, we wouldn't dare show our real selves.

Such a group, he says, offers love that's not unconditional but based on performance. That attitude does not model the love of Christ, which is what we desperately need.

A church that is "for show" also tends to blame and shame people when they fail. This church finds a scapegoat for its problems and attacks that person instead of talking and working things out, says Mains. These are probably ways our families of origin functioned. Such an assembly will smother, not foster growth.[4]

---

[3]Ibid., p. 8.
[4]Ibid., p. 8.

For quite a while, Billie didn't realize she was in an unhealthy church. "I loved it there and was deeply involved in ministry. But then I was divorced, and when I was hurting most, people in leadership turned against me. I had committed the 'unpardonable sin' and was shunned. It was terrible to go through divorce *and* lose my Christian family at the same time." She left that church and is now in a more healthy one.

Standing in Christ Alone

What do you do if an individual within a church where you are beginning to feel at ease and able to settle down nips at your heels?

Last Easter Sunday in a church I was visiting, a man who spoke briefly provided insight for such times by recalling an incident in his boyhood. Here's the gist of what he said:

"My brother and I weren't nice and poked at sea anemones on the beach with a stick. They'd close up and become hard.

"People poke sticks at us," he explained. "It happened to me. I asked God what to do about it. He said that there *would* be sticks poking. It happens. You need to attach yourself to the Rock. Then you'll become perceptive and know when to close up and protect yourself and when it's safe to be open."

Celia was relatively new in First Church when a woman decided to set her straight. "The reason you're having problems is your own fault." The woman went on to tick off attitudes and behaviors that she said were disobediences. "God will never bless you until you stop." Celia was stunned. Then she was devastated. Then she was confused. Then she was tempted to get out of that church and never come back.

Instead, she talked with a close Christian friend who'd been helping her. The two women looked at the facts. Did the other woman's point-of-view hold water? After thinking it through, they agreed it did not. Then they analyzed that woman's personality. "What's she like?"

"Extremely confrontive. Aggressive. Take charge."

"Does she represent the attitude of the church?"

"No. But at the time she intimidated me so I couldn't think rationally."

"So we can conclude that she's the one with the problem. You'll always meet people like that."

Over the next weeks, they discussed ways Celia could deflect such verbal blows by kindly but firmly stating her position and taking the same stance whenever necessary. They also agreed that Celia needn't leave the church.

Our Own Fear

It may not be *someone* who threatens to chase us out of our spiritual family home; it may be *something,* the way it was for Jo. When she felt that people were getting too close, she became frightened and left. Because of the Lord's intervention in a variety of ways, she grew stronger and more confident during the months ahead and decided to visit the group again. Now she was ready for greater closeness. She knows that her withdrawal earlier was not failure; it was simply a reflection of her stage of development then. When she says that it's really good to be back, her smile shines out from inside.

When Toby moved in with Debbie and learned to trust her because she proved trustworthy, he let her know unmistakably that he had no intention of bolting for life on the streets again. Not only did he have a kind mistress, he had a family and each gave love in a particular way. One sneaked treats to him under the table; another invited him on the bed at night; a third saw that he was defleaed and bathed.

It would be enough that a healthy church family helps our trust in God to grow, provides us with a sense of acceptance and belonging, and unfolds truth to our spirits from the Scriptures. But there's more. Through that family, God will heal by means of the gifts He has given individual members. "To each one the manifestation of the Spirit is given for the common good" (1 Corinthians 12:7).

The specific ability to encourage and speak wisdom comes *from the Counselor, the Holy Spirit of God himself.* It is actually God working through that individual in order to re-create us. So God has surprises for us hidden within some of our spiritual brothers and sisters. A word fitly spoken. Hospitality offered through invitations to lunch and dinner and a picnic, where we observe how a healthy family functions.

One noon across my kitchen table, Diane helped me see that my spiritual brothers and sisters are more than just individuals who have gifts. She leaned forward and sparkled with excitement as she spoke. "I was at work, sitting in a meeting, when God showed it to me. *People* are gifts.

"You need to get inside to see what they're like. Some are fragile. Some are double-wrapped. Some are wrapped in plain brown, or unattractive paper. I remember once being given a package that was badly wrapped and I supposed there couldn't be anything of value inside. But it was a beautiful piece of art."

Learning to see people themselves as gifts from God to me enables me to accept them. The confrontive, abrasive ones help me to be more confrontive myself. The shy, gentle ones who are double-wrapped force me out of myself so I can focus on their need.

Healing also comes when we see that God has manifested the Spirit through *us* for the common good. When we work in the nursery or help in the primary class, we reach outside ourselves and experience a measure of fulfillment because we are being contributive. *God is working through me.* Not that we work to gain plaudits the way we did before. But we do so through the energy that comes from the same Holy Spirit who gave us the gifts.

Even the most humble and damaged of us can give. Toby, with his scarred feet and body, reminds me of that every time he comes to visit, waggles a snaggle-toothed grin and jumps up on my lap, settles down with a sigh, and I am warmed to the core.

Thinking It Over

1. Do you identify with Toby? If so, how? What feelings have the two of you had in common?
2. If the author had interviewed you about your experiences for this chapter, what would you have told her? Your time in a dysfunctional church? Your search for an ideal church that doesn't exist? What changes in your thinking about church are you going to make?
3. Since church is family, what is your position in it right now? Separated? Attend but feel like an outsider? A silent family member? Warming up? Learning to take the initiative? Feel wholly accepted and part of family life? Do you feel satisfied with where you're at?
4. If someone "poked a stick at you" in a church, what would be the best way to handle the experience?
5. In what ways have individuals in the church helped you

on your journey? Where appropriate, write a note of thanks. Ask God to show you ways you can get out of yourself by "doing unto others." How will you begin to act on what He shows you?

11

Tough Times Are Teaching Times

Across from me on a shelf is a stuffed koala, hugging her baby. I am touched by the bondedness and love they depict. And in my spirit, I remember that God my Father enfolds me just that way.

To insure the koalas stay together, the manufacturer has attached them to each other. Mama perpetually hugs her baby with the help of Velcro. With God, there is no Velcro. God's *love* binds Him to me, as He assures, through Jeremiah:

I have loved you with an everlasting love; I have drawn you with lovingkindness. (31:3)

We know in our heads that we are cherished and encircled by the protective arm of our Father. Why do we tremble with fear when we think that God might be leading us into one more learning experience? Why are we so sure that it will most certainly be an *"ugh"* and not a *"wow"*?

Learning Does Not Equal Pain

Most of us expect learning experiences to *hurt,* and who doesn't want to avoid pain? We've hurt enough already. We're not masochists. We do want health, but we want it *without* more misery.

It's important to establish this firmly in our spirits: No matter what pain we have faced since the day we committed our healing to the Counselor, we have been under God's *protection.* One verse in the Bible, not often recognized as guaranteeing protection, is Titus 2:14. "To purify for himself a people that are *his very own*" (emphasis added).

The expression "his very own" (translated "peculiar people" in the King James Version) is translated from a Greek word that is made up of two words, one which means "around," or encircled, and the other which means "to be." It can be charted by a dot within a circle: As the circle is around the dot, so God is around each one of His beloved children.

"This is also a place of protection," writes Kenneth Wuest. I think of these things as I look at mama koala's encircling arms. No painful experience can penetrate God's protecting presence "except it go through the permissive will of God first."[1] That's the position in which we who have entrusted ourselves to the divine Physician live. Therefore, these are the "facts" we can rely on when feelings try to tell us otherwise.

Facts vs. Feelings

Fact Number One: Of all the healing methods that the Counselor prescribes, learning experiences are among the

---

[1]Kenneth S. Wuest, *Wuest's Word Studies in the Greek New Testament, Vol. III* (Grand Rapids, Mich.: Wm. B. Eerdmans Co., 1973), pp. 15–16.

most effective. "Truth, to be understood, must be lived," A. W. Tozer says emphatically, "Truth cannot aid us until we become participators in it."[2] It is not enough to *know the truth* that God loves and accepts us, for example. We must learn to allow that truth and not old distortions that we are unlovable to *determine our behavior.* That can happen only by experience.

During the kindergarten years of my inner healing, I *heard* the truth that God loved and accepted me. *Loved child of God* was my identity and on that I could base my self-image. As Tozer says, though, knowing is not enough. I had to embrace the truth and live by it.

So God gave me plenty of opportunity. John and I and our family had been living for about six months without a regular income. More and more, I became convinced that God wanted me to look for a job. *After seventeen years outside the secular workplace, Lord?*

Within a few weeks, I was hired as a clerk in a department store. Part of me shrank with fear at learning new things. I was sure I'd fail—make some stupid mistake and hear my supervisor announce: "That's it. You're through."

In my spirit, however, I could see footprints of a miracle. Not "water into wine," but a God-selected sequence of events. A center-stage miracle in which God produced a fairy-tale solution to my problem wouldn't have forced me to do the very things from which my unbiblical self-image recoiled. Because we needed the money, I had to conquer cash registers and paper work and intimidating customers by drawing on what I knew to be true: I was encircled with God's presence. He was with me and He would help me.

Gradually, as God intended, I became more confident. He led me to another more demanding job where my con-

---

[2]A. W. Tozer, *That Incredible Christian* (Harrisburg, Pa.: Christian Publications, 1964), pp. 92, 94.

fidence rose even more. I had to step out, stand up, and speak up and in doing so, began to develop into a woman I could respect.

Fact Number Two: Some learning experiences definitely are painful. Like most of us, I dug in my heels when it came to hard things. But more and more I became convinced that running from hard things was counterproductive. One way God impressed that on me was through Hebrews 12.

"Let us throw off every thing that hinders" (v. 1). *Yes. The old attitudes and behavior patterns that keep me an emotional child. I want to leave them behind.*

"Let us fix our eyes on Jesus . . . who . . . endured such opposition. . . . You have not resisted to the point of shedding your blood" (vv. 2–4). *God the Son himself is my role model. He willingly exposed himself to pain, torture, and death so I might be healed. He certainly didn't run from hard things. If He could do that, I, by His indwelling, overcoming presence, can do this.*

"Endure hardship as discipline; God is treating you as sons" (v. 7). *Discipline is training, not punishment. God is teaching me and correcting my mistakes so I can develop into the likeness of the second Adam. He allows hard things to come to me so He can Father me through them. I need to see learning experiences through my Father's eyes.*

"Therefore, strengthen your feeble arms and weak knees. Make level paths for your feet, so the lame may not be disabled, but rather healed" (vv. 12–13). *Exactly how I feel. Feeble arms hanging at my sides. Knees on the inside, wobbly and barely able to hold me up. Disabled. But the learning experiences God allows are like physical therapy, the kind I've watched my therapist friend Cindy apply to a patient. They may hurt, but they are opportunities for me to develop and mature with Father's help.*

I grasped those truths as tightly in my spirit as I could

and returned daily to hear them again and reaffirm my resolve. Hard things hurt because they threatened my thread-
bare ego. But the more I accepted—and finally even wel-
comed them as training by a loving Father and counted on
my Present Helper to go through them with me—the less
painful and intimidating they became and the more upbuild-
ing.

Fact Number Three: "Pain . . . is not God's great goof."[3]
It is because we are images of God that we feel pain. We
were created with an emotional nature because God himself
has emotions. That means we experience love and joy and
its dark side—anger and sorrow—the way He does. "[Pain]
is a gift—the gift that nobody wants," says Philip Yancy.[4]

One reason that it is a gift, Yancy reminds us, is that
pain lets us know something is wrong with us and needs
attention. We feel alone and as though pressed by heavy
weights; terrified as though facing a personal Armageddon.
Get help now.

Still, when we experience pain, we do ask ourselves: "If
God is truly in charge, somehow connected to all the world's
suffering, why is He so capricious, unfair? Is He the cosmic
Sadist who delights in watching us squirm?"[5]

Hardly. His attitude toward human suffering is most
clearly expressed in this: "God himself succumbed to pain."[6]
Physical, yes. But also emotional backs-of-the-hand when
He was called a liar and a blasphemer. Remember, that
happened to God himself.

Historically, mankind chose to live in a world in which
people were slammed by injustice and left bleeding when

---

[3]Philip Yancy, *Where Is God When It Hurts?* (Grand Rapids, Mich.: Zondervan Publishing House, 1977), p. 29.
[4]Ibid.
[5]Ibid., p. 63.
[6]Ibid., p. 161.

they chose rebellion against God instead of obedience. Had we not done so, we would never have had to experience the dark side of emotions.

God planned from the beginning to become a human and experience our pain so we could be healed. Not only that, but the Healer himself then comes to live in us to experience our personal, present pain and oversee and expedite our renewal.

So our misery is not because God is a cosmic Sadist. We *feel* because of who we *are*. God allows specific learning experiences to enter our lives because they can be used for healing. He doesn't cause them to happen. Some come because the disease of sin has distorted every part of every person who has ever been.

Other of our learning experiences are the result of our own mistakes. "I met this guy who needed mothering, and I was a world-class caretaker," a friend told me. "After I married him, he became extremely abusive; the more I tried to take care of him, the worse he got and the more he demanded. It was awful. I realize that marrying him was very foolish."

A third kind of learning experience moves in because God allows life to happen to us just as it happens to others. He may not keep a genetic disorder from being passed on to us or a mismanaging employer from taking away our source of income. Instead of functioning as a Magician in the Sky and sprinkling potential ouches with tinsel dust, He permits them and uses them to train us to take more initiative or to persevere.

Fact Number Four: Not all learning experiences are miserable, rotten, and devastating. Rather, some are like glimpses through a most favorite childhood toy, a kaleidoscope. These are surprise moments—flashes of insight. We smile with delight at the colors and forms.

One of these happened to me as I sat drinking tea in a shopping mall and watching people go by. Laughing, a couple about my own age approached an escalator that was coming down from the floor above. Instead of turning away embarrassed at their mistake at trying to board the wrong one, with hilarity they made exaggerated leaps in a mock effort to go up the down escalator before they finally gave up. *Like kids who need a scolding,* I thought first. Then, *Life need not always be so desperately serious. Let go. Have fun.*

Another took place on the lawn one summer day as I sat digging dandelions. In places, weeds had been previously dug up but had sprung up again. *They need to be killed at the roots.* Like old habits, they are fiercely determined. Slicing off the tops won't do. *The Counselor enables us to get at those deep roots.*

Hard things and insights of form and color and ordinary moments which become extraordinary will be interwoven into every woman's healing process by the Counselor. Our part is to recognize them and allow God to teach us what He means.

However, we aren't to suppose that He expects us to trudge down every rutted road—that we must *always* make the choice that exposes us to the most misery. "I see God as a deity who demands that I suffer. So I expect that He wants me to put up with this abuse now, so I'll learn from it."

If we are down on ourselves, we are liable to believe that God means us to be martyrs. The truth is that He doesn't mean for us to passively allow another to hurt and crush us "to teach us a lesson."

Hard Lessons, Loving God

God's hard lessons usually come without any viable choice on our part. Like the time I returned from a weekend away to find the sink stopped up and beyond a do-it-your-selfer's ability to fix it. No plumber was available for four days. My husband and son were sick. I had a writing assignment to get out. My choices were to run away from home (not a serious option), or to accept this as an opportunity to feel my anger and frustration, bring it to God, and see Him as ready to cultivate in me the confidence, determination, and ability I needed in order to cope. Definitely a learning experience.

Even so, hard learning experiences call out faith, because God doesn't hand us a blueprint up front: *Trust me,* He asks. And the only alternative is to scream and stamp our feet and shake our fist at heaven.

But we have already chosen to cooperate with the Healer at every turn, so even though we wail, we're obliged to abide by our commitment and choose to trust Him anyway. Down the road, we'll feel warm satisfaction over our choice. For, it is by having to trust that we learn to trust.

Here's how it happened to friends:

- "This woman I thought was my friend turned against me. She chewed me out royally. Because I've been feeling abandoned, this was very difficult for me. But through the experience, I came to see that other people are damaged too. It's not 'me' and 'them.' We're all in the same boat."
- "My husband had an affair. God didn't want that to happen, but since we are all sinners it did. I've had to stay very close to God to survive because I've been feeling so betrayed. I don't know what the future holds for my marriage. But I appreciate God and His faithfulness more than I did before this happened. My trust in Him has grown."
- "God made it possible for me to get an executive position. I'm a person who has found it difficult to make decisions because I don't trust my judgment. Here I am, having to

make all kinds of important decisions. My friend says that's God's way of showing me I've been devaluing myself, and He's helping me to see my potential."

A Mighty Grip on Eternal Truth

Jacob, whose father and mother played favorites and who took on the family's manipulating ways, was allowed to go through his own hard learning experience. Laban, his mother's uncle for whom he worked, turned out to be a world-class manipulator, scheming so that Jacob unwittingly married Leah and not Rachel, the woman he really loved. It took fourteen years as Laban's ranch hand before Jacob fulfilled his contract and Rachel could be his.

This was exactly the learning experience Jacob needed—long coming in our scale of time, short in terms of eternity. Although He didn't provide Jacob with a blueprint up front, He did make him a promise—the same one He makes to us. "I am with you and will watch over you wherever you go, and will bring you back to this land. I will not leave you until I have done what I have promised" (Genesis 28:15).

Jacob's experiences, however frustrating and exasperating, were allowed by God so that he would relinquish old ways and develop new, healthy ones. Like many women's experiences, Jacob's situation seemed interminable. But denial is broken slowly, and self-knowledge develops the same way.

There are no easy words for a woman who is doing what she knows God has for her by caring year after year for a crotchety parent or coping with a Peter Pan husband. *All learning times and no resting times, Lord?* Only the word that God gave Jacob: *I have a special purpose planned for you. To accomplish that purpose, we must travel this way first.*

These truths were impressed on me again through a passage in *Ben Hur,* Lew Wallace's fictional classic. A Jew born to comfort, Ben Hur became a Roman galley slave straining at the oars under inhuman conditions. Finally freed and later entered in the chariot race in competition with champions and the man determined to destroy him, he strained to win.

> Where got Ben Hur the large hand and mighty grip
> which helped him now so well?
> Where but from the oar with which
> so long he fought the sea?[7]

Learning experiences come so that we will develop a mighty grip. Always, through every experience, we are encircled with the nurturing, loving hands of God himself.

Thinking It Over

1. Read Titus 2:14. Illustrate for yourself Kenneth S. Wuest's teaching and draw a dot within a circle. Label the dot with your name and the circle "God." Notice that testing times have to go through the protective presence of God. How does that make you feel?
2. Have you expected God to change you through a supernatural experience? How has that expectation frustrated you? What new insights do you gain from Chapter 11?
3. Think about one or more learning experiences you've had that contributed toward your health and growth in some way. What were your feelings then? How do you feel about them now?
4. Ask God to keep you alert to the delightful "kaleidoscope" learning experiences He places in your life. Write to Him about them as they occur.
5. Review the principles in this chapter on learning expe-

---

[7]Lew Wallace, abridged edition by I.O. Evans, *Ben Hur* (N.Y.: Frederick Warne and Co. Inc., 1959), p. 156.

riences. Talk with God concerning any fears you have about facing these kinds of experiences. Reflect on Genesis 28:15. Keep choosing to be vulnerable before God, to count on His goodness and faith even though part of you isn't convinced. Keep reminding yourself that you are His very own, beloved daughter.

III

Now and Then

12

When It Hurts Most

The journey toward wholeness can be painful: We need a strategy, then, to keep the days more light than shadow. At times, the ordinary things of life will seem to take more than we have to give. Our emotions are so easily rattled, our will and resolve easily defused.

In the predawn, as John and I left New York for our first mission field 3,000 miles away in the state of Washington, we thought we had our strategy well-planned. Our two young sons were safely settled in the backseat; traveler's checks and an Automobile Association of America route were in the glove compartment.

But on the other side of the tunnel in New Jersey, our car developed a *gerthump* under the hood. The mechanic's verdict: a problem in the drive line. With no time to get the car fixed, we'd have to make the first half of our trip, to mission headquarters in Missouri, in a damaged car driving under thirty-two miles an hour.

The repairs done, we headed on to Washington. But now the transmission wouldn't stay in high gear unless John held on to the shift for dear life. Hold on he did—across the steeps of the Rocky Mountains and the seemingly endless desert and into the lush Pacific Northwest. He felt as though his hand was welded to the gear shift.

One thing we learned: When you have to make a journey in a damaged vehicle, you need a *survival strategy.*

A New Plan

Years later, I found myself *gerthumping* along on another kind of journey—this one to emotional wholeness. Only when I found myself wanting to go to bed for the rest of my life did I realize that I needed a better "plan" than that. It had to include every part of me: physical, mental, emotional, social, volitional, and spiritual. The same is true for you. Let's take a look at such a plan.

The Physical: Restoration for us humans takes place all along our journey, not during a few hours in a garage. But because the process is gradual and we must live with ger-thumps and plunks in the meantime, doing so can be tough on our chassis. In my case, tension collected in the back of my neck until it became stiff and painful. I developed insomnia. Other women tell me they develop pounding headaches and stomach problems. "I went to the doctor with chest pains, fearful that I was having a heart attack, and he said it was nerves."

As I have said, my psychologist friend often recommends clients have a physical checkup both to uncover physical causes for emotional problems and to treat physical reactions to emotional upsets. The trouble is, when we strongly dislike ourselves, we're not motivated to go to the doctor or to take care of ourselves. Besides that, when our bodies throb here and ache there or we're heavy with depression, we have neither the energy nor the will to do that.

All we want during down times is to gorge on chips or

not eat until a week from Friday; to sit like a slug in front of the TV; choose from our closet the oldest, most sagging pair of jeans and the sweater with the baggy elbows. *Life doesn't matter. I don't matter.*

What we need is to take the initiative to practice health. If the motivation doesn't seem to exist within us, we may need a helping friend to get us started. "Can I make myself accountable to you for now to take better care of myself? Will you check on me regularly and encourage me to keep doing better and show me how?"

Melanie knew that she needed to eat breakfast and have more than a cookie and coffee for lunch the way she tended to do. She also knew that she needed to exercise regularly and felt better when she did that. But she didn't seem able to make herself do so consistently, so each week her friend and mentor asked Melanie what she'd been eating and whether or not she'd been walking daily the way she'd decided and if she'd had that physical checkup. Melanie told her friend, "Because I know you're going to ask me, I'm much more liable to do it."

The I-don't-matter mind-set can be our worst enemy. "It's Jesus first, others second, and me last," women have told me over the years.

"That statement is a grand oversimplification," I point out. "Of course, we should want Jesus' will above all else, and His will is that we care about people. But we are not to neglect ourselves. That's absolutely wrong and against God's will."

We have been entrusted by God with wonderfully created bodies. No matter how decimated, they are priceless and we are to respect and care for them. Besides, our bodies are temples, just as much as that sparkling, grandly constructed and appointed Old Testament building was. In a flesh-and-blood way, the grandeur of our own matches the one that existed in Jerusalem. "Do you not know that your body is a temple of the Holy Spirit, who is in you, whom you have received from God?" (1 Corinthians 6:19).

To remain strong—especially under emergency conditions—flesh-and-blood temples need nourishment from the five food groups, rest, and exercise to work off emotional energy, not gold leaf and velvet. A female temple needs to work at looking her best (that helps her *feel* better). And she needs to have *fun* regularly—whether it is half an hour with a good book or savoring frozen yogurt at the mall. Without these, we've sabotaged our progress. When women do start to take care of themselves, I remind them that this is a sign they are on their way upward.

A vow to practice these and other disciplines perfectly from this day on simply won't work, though. Instead, we need to embrace the Alcoholics Anonymous tenet and work our program "a day at a time."

The Mental. As we've seen and experienced for ourselves on our way to healing, the inside of our head seems to be in chaos. Replays of conversations, self-recriminations, vituperations, regrets, and self-pityings tumble and bump against one another. In my own mind, mobs of words were elbowing their way, bruising as they went. Outwardly, I looked as fine as a car of ours that sat in the driveway. Its paint job and upholstery were unmarred; but under the hood was a different matter.

Prayer helps immeasurably. So does journaling. But a third way to cope can become like soothing waters rinsing our soul.

It did for Lorraine, whose mental confusion was spilling out her mouth. She spoke in fragments of sentences and jumped from subject to subject.

I gave her a fact sheet I'd written titled "How to Rest,"

outlining what I'd learned when I was at her stage. "Practicing rest in Christ during our journey is an essential emergency treatment," I explained. "Once you get into the habit, you'll want to make it part of your lifestyle from here to eternity."

She did as I recommended, sat down and took deep breaths and relaxed her body—beginning with her feet and working her way up to her head. Then, for the next several minutes she focused on the living God. *Lord. You are here, living in me.* She found that this exercise created in her pockets of mental ease.

When we're quieter within, we are more able to extend that place by choosing to see beauty in our present moment and fasten on that. The green of the grass out our window; the roses blooming across the street. God *wants* to show them to us.

Besides the unexplored beauty that graces our lives, focusing on the presence of God as we perform the task of the moment—from filing our nails to making our beds—creates mental calm.

The principle to keep remembering every step of the way is this: When our minds have a focal point, inner chaos is more easily brought under control. When that focus is God and His Word, truth can permeate to our core.

Choose pithy phrases of promise and hope. Center on them, breathe them as prayers as you walk through your days.

David's declaration: "The Lord is my shepherd" (Psalm 23:1).

Christ's invitations: "Come to me. . . . I will give you rest" (Matthew 11:28).

"Whoever comes to me I will never drive away" (John 6:37).

The apostles' strong statements: "God is love" (1 John 4:16).

"The Father himself loves you" (John 16:27).

"He will keep you strong to the end" (1 Corinthians 1:8).

The Emotional. At various periods during the journey, over and over I've had to assure myself and other women that their feelings are normal. "You were sexually abused beginning at age five? How else would you feel but angry?" "Your father said he loved you but left home and never came back? How else would you feel but abandoned and devastated?"

We may know intellectually that emotion is "an experience or mental state characterized by a strong degree of feeling,"[1] and that it is "a healthy mechanism, designed to protect us,"[2] but that doesn't make us like the inner push-pull any better. Anger, abandonment, and devastation *hurts.*

Since emotions are normal human responses, to feel our feelings is part of the healing process. Along the way when new insights come or something causes old pain to return, we may need to grieve, to feel our anger—not endlessly—but so we can go on. Doing so is healthy and it is Christian. So whenever we feel ourselves pressed down or churned up again, it's time to ask ourselves, "What am I feeling? Where are these feelings coming from?"

The next step is to do as we have before: Keep expressing those feelings in the acceptable ways that have been described. *I want to deal with it, be healed, and go on to live constructively.*

No shame repressed my two-year-old grandson when he told Mommy what scared him. There was the man's face on a commercial, and Linda when she got a pie in the face on Sesame Street. He felt afraid and he said so. Mommy, he

---

[1] Clyde M. Narramore, *The Psychology of Counseling* (Grand Rapids, Mich.: Zondervan, 1960), p. 279.

[2] Dr. John White, *Changing on the Inside* (Ann Arbor, Mich.: Servant Publications, 1991), p. 128.

knew, was his comforter. And God the Holy Spirit is ours. He is present in us day by day to hear our emotional turmoil and help us manage it.

One way He does that is to provide opportunities for us to get the reassuring hugs a mommy gives her child—in acceptable ways, of course. It's our responsibility to let our healing helpers know what we need. At one point, I wore a twenty-five-cent gold-colored heart those times and told my husband that it meant I needed love.

To keep our spirits up, it's urgent that we identify what helps us and then build it into our lives. Music. Playing with the cat. Digging in the flower beds. Painting a picture. Writing a poem.

The point is that we can count on the Counselor to help us deal with every ebb and flow of emotion and to direct us to constructive mood-changing activities. Instead of being swept away by these feelings, He wants to help us learn to manage them and go on to live life with and in Him.

One of the most important discoveries we'll make during the process is that "the peace of God, which transcends all understanding, will guard your hearts" (Philippians 4:7). That is, as we focus on God through the painful times, in our spirit, which is a dimension that is deeper than our emotional nature, we'll sense His strength.

That's what Paul implies in the following statement. "We are hard pressed on every side, but not crushed; perplexed, but not in despair; persecuted, but not abandoned; struck down, but not destroyed" (2 Corinthians 4:8–9). *In the flesh I am pained; in the Spirit, I have hope.*

The Social. Babe, my grandfather's dog, hid under the porch every spring after his annual clipping. Lying on my belly, I'd plead with him to come out, but his only response was to stare at me with eyes full of humiliation and shame.

Eventually, an empty stomach did what I could not.

We, too, may opt for the seclusion of under-the-porch when we plod through new valleys. But doing so only intensifies feelings of rejection and isolation, humiliation and shame. What we must do is keep making our way out into company with those we trust.

God will draw us to such people if we ask. These are in addition to the ones involved in our healing process. One emotional day, I needed someone, and as I looked to God, I thought of a former co-worker. Despite my lack of energy, I made arrangements to go to lunch with her. I never mentioned how I was feeling nor asked her for strokes. Just by being with her, I left encouraged because she's that kind of Christian.

Do we have a right to stay away from critical, destructive people—at least for now? Of course. Some of them we may not be able to avoid, but we can confront them about their behavior. If they're unable or unwilling to change now, God will provide us with the grace to accept them as they are. He'll show us other, healthy ways to find companionship.

Keep edging further and further into socialization. A few words to a familiar grocery clerk. To a pewmate. Cultivate a new acquaintance at a women's Bible study. Volunteer at the hospital or charity thrift store or the church. Take an art or craft class and get to know other women. Secular or ministry-oriented, social contacts keep you from becoming ingrown.

As you relate to others, you'll make a couple of amazing discoveries. *These women aren't so different from me. They're struggling, too—in their own ways. By contributing to someone else's life I'm strengthening my own.* "I'll show you how to do a half-double crochet." "I'd be glad to drive you to the doctor's." *I have something to give.*

Volitional. Now is the time for all women to cultivate their will. Since Eve, God has given us the ability and the right to make personal choices. Whether to walk for our health or watch a TV soap. Whether to focus on the presence of God this moment or on life's inequities.

As often as necessary, go back to the decision you made at the head of your pilgrimage: *God my Counselor, I have already chosen to trust you no matter how tough it gets. I know you are in charge and are acting in a way to produce my healing. I choose to persist in spite of the pain.*

Doing that may make us sweat because we're sick and tired of sharp turns and dead ends. Or because we're not good at making choices. Period.

Earlier, I tried to only make choices that would please people. Anyway, since I was a Christian, didn't God want me to not make my own choices? Didn't He want to over-power me with His will and give me the strength to carry it through?

That is not His plan. He created me with a will and regenerated it when I was born again. My responsibility was to retrain the will I'd given away by making small choices. Which restaurant did I want to go to? Which TV show did I want to watch? Every time, I gained experience in healthy choosing.

As I began doing that, I was able to begin to make choices that contributed to my inner healing in spite of the way I felt at the moment. I was able to choose to do His will. My will need not be controlled by my emotions.

The Spiritual. Stick to God like a barnacle to a rock. No matter how confused about Him you may be or how much you feel like a failure as a Christian. "Come to me," He urges. He doesn't mean for you to wait until after you get rid of your anger or doubt. Stay attached to Him because you are counting on who you know *He* is and what you know *He* has promised.

"Never will I leave you;
never will I forsake you." (Hebrews 13:5)

Ask Him for small, encouraging experiences and keep your eyes and your heart open for them.

"God showed me something through a Bible teacher on the radio the other day. . . ."

"God gave me the opportunity to feel warm and loved when my toddler granddaughter hugged my neck . . ."

"I walked on the beach and saw in the ocean a picture of God's power."

Keep talking to God about every facet of life as you live it, because He is your daddy. The kind you've ache for. Never forget that healing comes by living in relationship with Him.

"I can't believe that's all God wants from me right now," a woman told me stunned. "Just to have a relationship with Him." She'd supposed He'd been tapping his foot waiting for her to straighten up; then they could be close. Like many of us, she'd internalized wrong ideas about God's requirements for her and His expectations of her. *Be self-sacrificing, perfectly pure inside and out.*

The more she cultivated her relationship with God by being with Him this moment and then the next, the more she began to understand that's what God wants first of all. "Walk with me; abide in me; trust in me, love me." As we relate the moments of our lives to God, we *are* beginning to live in love.

Abiding

By attending to these areas of our lives, we are able to push beyond the pain. God provides the strength—not in a grand rush of heavenly power—but moment by moment, the way sap flows from vine to branch as we learn to abide in God.

Part of our responsibility is to cultivate the determination to keep on, the way athletes do—carefully pushing beyond the pain. Pioneers traveling west on the overland trail had to do that too. So does the natural world during every frozen season.

We women are able to push beyond the pain here, now, on this journey because we are joined with God. So cultivate your relationship with Him. For it's in your spiritual dimension that you overcome. "We are more than conquerors through him who loved us" (Romans 8:37).

Thinking it Over

1. Is it possible that physical problems like insomnia, PMS menopausal symptoms, or lack of energy could contribute to the way you feel now? Have you had a medical checkup? Why is putting it off self-defeating?

2. Think through again the way to rest. If you haven't integrated it into your lifestyle, make a thirty-day experiment and see what it does for you.

3. What does it mean to you to feel your feelings, express them, be healed from them, and go on? What activities like listening to or making music or creating something artistic are helpful emotional releases for you?

4. Have you, like Babe, tended to hide under the porch? What constructive opportunities for socialization that feel right for you now do you have?

5. Have you been a people pleaser? Been afraid to make choices for fear they'll be wrong? Think of small choices

you can make now trusting in God's insight to cultivate your God-given will.

6. How does it feel to call God "Daddy"? Journal a brief description of Father God as you've supposed Him to be and another as you're discovering that He is.

13

Celebrate and Anticipate

Like children checking their growth charts for added inches, most women under reconstruction usually don't think they're growing fast enough. Great as it sounds, double-time development, like Jack's overnight beanstalk, is definitely not the norm—not even a good idea.

It certainly wasn't for Robert Wadlow. At age five he was 5 feet 4; at age eleven, 6 feet 7. By the time he was twenty-two, he measured 8 feet 11.1 inches and was featured as The Tallest Man in the World in Ringling Brothers and Barnum & Bailey Circus.

The cause for this real-life giant's streak upward was an overactive pituitary gland. As a result, he had an extremely fragile bone structure and was threatened with permanent injury by every fall. Eventually, he had to use a cane when he walked and, tragically, at twenty-two years of age, he died.[1]

In every area of life, how much stronger, healthier is the growth that comes slowly. Growth, after all, is "gradual development toward maturity." And development is "a step

---

[1] Frederick Drimmer, *Born Different* (N.Y.: Athenium, 1988), p. 70.

or a stage in growth."[2] The shoot first, then the stalk, single leaf, clusters of leaves, buds and blossoms. When each develops in its time, the plant will be sturdy.

Wrong Comparisons

We may be in a hurry because we're comparing ourselves to *those other* women. They are the ones who seem self-assured, have dazzling smiles and a ready wit in roomfuls of people. *I'm not like that. What's more, I'll never be like that.*

If "successful" women are our measuring stick, we're gauging our growth wrongly. For one thing, they may not be as damage-free as we think, only as good at projecting an image as we may have been. So we may be measuring against a false standard.

The person against whom to measure yourself is *you,* and not someone else. An experience from childhood helps us see that more clearly. During those years, some of us were measured back to back with an adult. During those years, it seemed no use: we'd never catch up with mom/dad/big brother/grandpa.

How much better was the other way of charting our growth. In this method, we were lined up against the wall or doorjamb, and a pencil mark was made just above our heads. "See how much you've grown since last time!"

Every child grows at her own rate. We are not like babies at the pediatrician for a checkup, measured and categorized in the percentile where we fit compared to other babies our age. And so, a word of caution:

Many of us are in a hurry to grow because of our *expectations* of ourselves. Perfectionistic to the last, we may be measuring ourselves according to an internal "ten." Therefore, we're not recognizing personal development when it

---

[2]*Webster's New World Dictionary*, Third College Edition (S & S Trade, 1988).

happens. If our perception of what God expects of us is inaccurate because we're still seeing Him as an impatient Universal Monarch, we may be shutting out His approval at the steps we've taken as well.

Wrong Ideas of Spiritual Perfection

It's vital to keep in mind that, while God is perfect, He recognizes that we are human. He *expects* us to grow, not jump to wholeness in one leap. Not to become Christlike in a week. Of course, Jesus is our pattern. But the technique to conform us to His image is more like sculpting than baking gingerbread men.

It's imperative to recognize our own personal growth when it takes place so we'll have the courage to keep on. Be encouraged by every speck of progress. Celebrate each one. Without accusing yourself, pinpoint areas to commit to your divine Physician for more work and cooperate with Him. There *will* be more work, for as we have seen, growth *is* a process for all of us. Periodically, review the following to see where you've been and where you are now.

- *Once I didn't know or wouldn't admit that "Something's wrong with me."*
  Now I have faced that fact. Finally I admitted to myself that going to bed depressed most nights wasn't right. I had a problem.
- *Once I thought that I'd just have to fumble along this way.* I didn't think there was any help for me. I was so ashamed to be an out-of-whack Christian that I couldn't tell anyone.
  Now I have told someone. I've told God. I've taken the risk and confessed what's inside me. Never did I think I could do that because I was sure He'd turn away. But He hasn't

done that. He's let me know that He's here and that He cares.

- *Once I thought it was up to me to fix myself.* Wasn't that what God expected? Finally I had to admit that I couldn't fix myself. I needed help desperately.

  Now I know that my help comes from God. He's the Divine Counselor and overseer of my inner healing. I have committed myself to Him to take charge of the process. He'll make it possible for me to find people and activities to help me. No matter how much I procrastinate and want to forget the whole idea, I stand by my commitment to do what He shows me. Above all, I can count on His merciful kindness to give me strength.

- *Once I depended on coping mechanisms to survive.* Eating. Having affairs. Doing sacrificial Christian things legalistically.

  Now I am seeing those practices as self-defeating. Instead of depending on them, I'm determined to loosen my grip on them.

- *Once I couldn't trust God.* Not really. That's because I pictured Him like the demanding, abusive authority figure who's had control over me. Besides, He let bad things happen to me. So how could I trust Him?

  Now I'm in the process of changing my perspective. That means seeing the same scene and its actors from another point of view. That idea was illustrated by a browser at our garage sale. She picked up a large flat stone on which one of my sons had painted a design and told her companion, "Oh, look. A pet rock." *You could call it that, couldn't you?* I thought.

  The new perspective I'm heading toward? *God is not like the father who abandoned, neglected, or abused me. He is just and loving.*

- *Once I repressed my feelings or was overwhelmed and controlled by them.* They were like a roiling, internal sea churning up the silt bottom and tossing debris on the shore.

Now I am learning to name and express my feelings and not allow them to control my life. When I feel powerless and guilty and controlled and close to tears, I ask myself, "What's going on here?" Then I know I can trace my feelings back to their cause and do something constructive about them.

- *Once I didn't know how to speak appropriately about the experiences that damaged me.* I've vacillated between wanting to tell everything to everyone and nothing to anyone.

  Now I'm learning boundaries. I'm sensing when it's timely to say "I've been struggling with my emotions because . . . and one thing I've learned is . . ." and when it's not timely. More and more, my intuition about this is firming up.

  Remember that even one positive change is growth. Have you admitted, "Something's wrong with me?" Told God? Are you counting on Him as Counselor? Are you stepping timidly but persistently toward faith in Him? Committing to Him just one need so He can prove His trustworthiness?

  Every time you deal constructively with your feelings and every time you refrain from telling your insides or taking the initiative to speak up—whichever you sense is the right action—is a growth point. Each time you cooperate with God at a particular change point, you shoot upward another millimeter.

- *Once I saw myself as a failure.* "It must be my fault that my dad was abusive toward me. I'm no good. I'm a loser."

  Now I'm learning to place blame where it belongs. It wasn't my fault that my father treated me the way he did. I do take responsibility for the immoral ways I chose to look for love as a substitute.

- *Once I saw myself only as a victim—used and abused—*"alone, confused, depressed, and sometimes as if [I were] going crazy."[3]

---

[3]Dan B. Allender, "When Trust is Lost," (Grand Rapids, Mich.: Radio Bible Class, 1992), p. 1.

Now I'm learning that, although I was a victim, Christ can provide the grace and power to make my painful past the foundation for a constructive future. "He understands your pain, because He too was a victim . . . He pathetically cried, 'My God, my God, why have You forsaken Me?' . . . Three days later, this victim of our sin rose from the dead to live His life through all who in surrender would trust Him."[4]

- *Once I saw myself as inferior.* Here's how I put it: "Rejection was an ugly rawboned intruder who elbowed her way into my teens demanding the front row of my life. . . . Year after year I sat where she taught me that I belonged, in the far corners."[5]

Now I am coming to see myself as a person of worth who is highly prized by God. "God's love was a fragile, chiffon truth that I fingered tenderly . . . *Look at me! God loves me.*"[6]

- *Once I pretended to be someone I was not.* "Yes, I'm fine, thank you." A stick-on smile kept ready for any occasion.

Now I'm learning to be an integrated person. Instead of living only by what I *feel,* I'm also considering what I think, what I believe about God, and what I can choose to do. All these components make up who I *am.* The more I act out of my integrated self, the more whole I am becoming.

- *Once I ran from intimacy with God.* While I craved it, still any kind of closeness scared me badly.

Now I am opening up to God. The doctrine of God living in a believer is no longer mere theology. It is truth by which I'm learning to live. The Spirit of the Son is my Divine Companion; He is life and grace; He will fill and empower me. In my spirit, we are one.

---

[4]Ibid, p. 23–24.
[5]Marion Duckworth, *The Greening of Mrs. Duckworth* (Wheaton, Ill.: Tyndale House, 1980), p. 16.
[6]Ibid, p. 87.

The Right View of You

Is the self-portrait inside your head subtly changing from failure, victim, and reject to winner, survivor-thriver, and accepted one? Are you just a whit more integrated, living out of your whole self and not just one part? A whisper more able to be yourself? A wink more convinced that His arms are open, His love extended?

With what issues do you need to deal now? Which attitudes and behavior patterns do you need to take to God? Every step forward will encourage you to trust Him to help you in the future as He has in the past.

Laura, who experienced years of parental abuse told me, "I know I'm making progress. I like myself more. I'm more comfortable being 'me' with a roomful of people and not worrying about what they think. Sure, I have a long way to go, but *I know I'm on my way.*"

So growth will keep happening, she also knows she has to make herself accountable to practice the healing disciplines God has shown her.

Kathy's childhood was icy. "I know now that the reason I was treated that way was not because of something in *me.* It was because my parents were damaged. Now, I don't blame myself. The past two years, I've grown more at peace in many ways."

As I personally look back over my own journey, I am astounded. Through the power of God, by the grace of God and the means of God, He has done a good work in me (Philippians 1:6).

My open wounds have been healed. Scars remain. They are similar to the patriarchs' piles of stones to remind me of the miracles that the Re-creator has worked in my life.

These are like the scar I bear from surgery over thirty-five years ago that repaired my female organs so I could bear children. When I run my fingers over the ridge it left in my flesh, I am reminded that it was as a result of the surgeon's knife that my womb has borne fruit. The scar on my abdomen no longer pains me when I touch it, for it is healed. Neither do I relive the pain of the past when I am reminded of the experiences of the past. But I do remember. And because I remember, I identify with others and can bear fruit.

My inner scars enable me to care because I've looked in windows from my own silent and shivering place and heard the laughter. I *know* because I've experienced the shame of lecherous hands groping my child body. I *know* because I've lingered in the shadows feeling helpless and hopeless and without a voice.

Our Counselor Never Fails

Your raw wounds will be healed too if, despite periodic, desperate urges to give up, you stand by your commitment to your Counselor. Trust and follow His directive. The scars that remain—that sensitize you to women wandering in pain—will be ones for which you will be wholeheartedly grateful. Because of them you will bear fruit.

Wounded women tell me that's what they want most: to help others like themselves. *Don't run ahead of God, trying to fix the world simply because it's in such bad shape.* Let Him show you when you're ready.

Then you'll encounter a woman in pain. She'll touch that inner scar and you'll respond out of the well of compassion that has been forming in you. It may be that you'll strike up a conversation with a strange woman the way Ellen did. "She was hurting and miserable. I understood and cared and said so. Then I told her why I could identify and how I found the way to healing. We exchanged phone numbers and have been in touch."

The healed do become the healers. That's God's goal for each wounded woman. He says so plainly:

Praise be to the God and Father of our Lord
Jesus Christ,
    The Father of compassion and the God of
       all comfort,
Who comforts us in all our troubles,
    so that we can comfort those in any trouble
       with the comfort we ourselves have received
         from God.
For just as the sufferings of Christ flow over into
    our lives,
so also through Christ our comfort overflows.
(2 Corinthians 1:3–5)

For now, you may feel like the primrose I planted outside our front door several years ago. In the spring it had bloomed sweetly, but winter had come and temperatures had dropped. A stub of a plant with sagging leaves forlorn in the barren flower bed, I glanced at it on my way out. *Dig it up,* I told myself. *No hope for it.*

I didn't get around to doing that. A week or two later, on my way out again, I glanced its way. *Nestled among its pathetic leaves were violet flowers.*

At the very time new growth seemed hopeless to me, inside that plant were the tracing of buds. Despite gray skies and frigid temperatures, *they blossomed.* And so will you.

Because I have walked through the chasm of emptiness, because I have listened to and watched the growth of many other women who have journeyed on the same path, I offer finally this prayer from the apostle Paul. Read it slowly and carefully. Read it often.

It is not an abject plea—far from it! It holds surety,

hope, the promise of fullness, where once there was only a void. Make it your prayer now, and always:

> I kneel before the Father, from whom his whole family, in heaven and on earth derives its name. I pray that out of his glorious riches he may strengthen you with power through his Spirit in your inner being, so that Christ may dwell in your hearts through faith. And I pray that you, being rooted and established in love, may have power, together with all the saints, to grasp how wide and long and high and deep is the love of Christ, and to know this love that surpasses knowledge—that you may be filled to the measure of all the fullness of God. (Ephesians 3:14–19)

I know that He alone is able—and I know He will complete the task. Rest in that promise!

Thinking it Over

1. How have you felt about your growth? If you've been measuring it wrongly, what changes are you setting out to make in the future? Against whom is it wisest to measure yourself?
2. List each step of progress toward healing you've made as described in this chapter. Take time to feel good about each and thank the Counselor for His intercession.
3. What are some areas in which you anticipate new growth? Why can you have confidence that this will take place?
4. Describe the difference between wounds and scars. What scars do you expect to carry with you? Why is it that they can be valuable?

5. In what ways would you like God to use your pain constructively?
6. Copy 2 Corinthians 1:3–5 on a 3 × 5 card. Put it where you'll see it often so its truth will become your solid stepping stones day by day.